The Pen~~guin Book of~~

THE SONNET

500 Years of a Classic Tradition in English

EDITED BY PHILLIS LEVIN

PENGUIN BOOKS

PENGUIN BOOKS

Published by the Penguin Group
Penguin Books Ltd, 80 Strand, London WC2R ORL, England
Penguin Putnam Inc., 375 Hudson Street, New York, New York 10014, USA
Penguin Books Australia Ltd, Ringwood, Victoria, Australia
Penguin Books Canada Ltd, 10 Alcorn Avenue, Toronto, Ontario, Canada M4V 3B2
Penguin Books India (P) Ltd, 11, Community Centre, Panchsheel Park, New Delhi – 110 017, India
Penguin Books (NZ) Ltd, Private Bag 102902, NSMC, Auckland, New Zealand
Penguin Books (South Africa) (Pty) Ltd, 24 Sturdee Avenue, Rosebank 2196, South Africa

Penguin Books Ltd, Registered Offices: 80 Strand, London WC2R ORL, England

First published in the USA in Penguin Books 2001
First published in Great Britain in Penguin Books 2001
1

Selection and Preface copyright © Phillis Levin, 2001

Set in 9/11.25 pt PostScript Adobe Sabon
Typeset by Rowland Phototypesetting Ltd, Bury St Edmunds, Suffolk
Printed in England by Clays Ltd, St Ives plc

ISBN 0-713-99529-7

CONTENTS

[v]

PREFACE

The sonnet is a monument of praise, a field of play, a chamber of sudden change. In its limited space it has logged, from the start, the awakening of a rational being to an overwhelming force in the self or the world. Its legacy of fourteen lines offers myriad challenges and opportunities, ranging from the technical to the spiritual. As a highly focused form, the sonnet attracts contradictory artistic impulses: in choosing and succumbing to the form, the poet agrees to follow the rules of the sonnet, but that willing surrender releases creative energy. From its origins in the thirteenth century Sicilian court of Frederick II to its English metamorphosis in the court of Henry VIII, the sonnet has recorded the unceasing conflict between the law of reason and the law of love, the need to solve a problem that cannot be resolved by an act of will, yet finds its fulfillment, if not its solution, only in the poem. Thematically and structurally, this tension plays itself out in the relationship between a fixed formal pattern and the endless flow of feeling.

The easiest thing to say about a sonnet is that it is a fourteen-line poem with a particular rhyme scheme and a particular mode of organizing and amplifying patterns of image and thought; and that, if written in English, the meter of each line usually will be iambic pentameter. But fourteen lines do not guarantee a sonnet: it is the behavior of those lines in relation to each other—their choreography—that identifies the form. There are two basic types of sonnets, the Italian (Petrarchan) and the English (Shakespearean); at least that is what we say in retrospect. In truth, by the time Petrarch and Shakespeare met the sonnet, each in his own era, its form was already prevalent, an excessively imitated fashion. Their names are thereby associated with specific patterns that they perfected but did not themselves invent.

Whatever its outward appearance, by virtue of its infrastructure the sonnet is asymmetrical. Opposition resides in its form the way load and support contend in a great building. Being dialectical, the sonnet is divided by nature: its patterns of division multiply perspective and meaning. The two types of sonnets, the Italian or Petrarchan and the English or Shakespearean, have each spurred variations, which renew the form from within. But each is built on an essential structure, a basic armature or template. In the Italian sonnet, lines are arranged in a rhyme pattern that makes the poem fall into two unequal sections, an octave rhyming abba abba and a sestet rhyming cdc dcd or cde cde (or some variation of those three rhymes). The *volta*, initiating a "turn" or change in tone, mood, voice, tempo, or perspective—a shift in focus, a swerve in logic, a change of heart, a moment of grace—occurs after the eighth line, or in the space between the eighth and ninth lines, which in many cases is indicated by a blank space on the page. Binary forces are still at work in the clear-cut divisions of the English sonnet, whose symmetrical quatrains precede a keen terminal couplet calling so much attention to itself that we forgot the tide began to change somewhat earlier. For though the *volta* occurs much later on in the space of an English sonnet, a significant rhetorical shift often appears after the eighth line, anticipating the more unmistakable change that will ensue, setting up in advance a very different method of closure while looking back to its predecessor.

The rhyming couplet, the most obvious innovation marking the difference between Petrarchan and Shakespearean sonnets, is even more surprising in light of the rhyme scheme that precedes it. The English sonnet is made of a succession of three quatrains arranged in a pattern called "alternating" or "open" rhyme, followed by a closing couplet: abab cdcd efef gg. As we well know from Shakespeare's sonnets, these four-line units have the potential to build to a momentum that will fulfill itself in the rhyming couplet of the final two lines, whose force and wit must close the poem convincingly, maintaining a separate identity by virtue of their radical (within the system of the sonnet) departure from the pattern of the preceding lines. The metrical limit of the iambic pentameter line contributes to the paradox of the sonnet, where formal structures elicit spontaneous gestures, artifice produces colloquial rhythm, and inherited patterns summon idiomatic speech.

This anthology is really an autobiography, not of any one person, but of the life of a literary form that ever since its conception has given birth—or rebirth—to many poetic identities, and to countless poems. The sonnets collected on these pages belong to a community whose borders keep shifting, and whose uniquely defined constitution makes "contraries meet in one" (Donne). The sonnet is a room for sounding these "contraries" and making sense of them, and for registering the edge of experience, in which passion and reason somehow lead to an inward transformation, experienced silently yet surfacing in language that points to a border beyond which language cannot go. It brings us, perhaps, to a place where both the poet and the reader must lose themselves to find themselves, where lovers in the labyrinth begin, in the words of Mary Wroth, "to leave all, and take the thread of love."

Proem

FRANCESCO PETRARCA

Canzoniere, 132

S' amor non è, che dunque è quel ch' io sento?
ma s' egli è amor, per Dio, che cosa et quale?
se bona, ond' è l'effetto aspro mortale?
se ria, ond' è sì dolce ogni tormento?

S' a mia voglia ardo, ond' è 'l pianto e lamento?
s' a mal mio grado, il lamentar che vale?
O viva morte, o dilettoso male,
come puoi tanto in me s' io nol consento?

Et s' io 'l consento, a gran torto mi doglio.
Fra sì contrari venti in frale barca
mi trovo in alto mar senza governo,

sì lieve di saver, d' error sì carca
ch' i' medesmo non so quel ch' io mi voglio,
e tremo a mezza state, ardendo il verno.

GEOFFREY CHAUCER

from *Troilus and Criseyde*

Canticus Troili

"If no love is, O God, what fele I so?
And if love is, what thing and which is he?
If love be good, from whennes cometh my woo?
If it be wikke, a wonder thynketh me,
When every torment and adversite
That cometh of hym, may to me savory thinke,
For ay thurst I, the more that ich it drynke.

"And if that at myn owen lust I brenne,
From whennes cometh my waillynge and my pleynte?
If harm agree me, wheto pleyne I thenne?
I noot, ne whi unwery that I feynte.
O quike deth, O swete harm so queynte,
How may of the in me swich quantite,
But if that I consente that it be?

"And if that I consente, I wrongfully
Compleyne, iwis. Thus possed to and fro,
Al stereless withinne a boot am I
Amydde the see, bitwixen wyndes two,
That in contrarie stonden evere mo.
Allas! what is this wondre maladie?
For hete of cold, for cold of hete, I dye."

[*after the Italian of Petrarch's* Canzoniere, *132*]

The Penguin Book of
THE SONNET

SIR THOMAS WYATT

"The longe love, that in my thought doeth harbar"

The longe love, that in my thought doeth harbar
    And in myn hert doeth kepe his residence
    Into my face preseth with bold pretence,
    And therin campeth, spreding his baner.
She that me lerneth to love and suffre
    And will that my trust, and lustes negligence
    Be reinèd by reason, shame, and reverence
    With his hardines taketh displeasure.
Wherewithall, unto the hertes forrest he fleith,
    Leving his entreprise with payne and cry
    And there him hideth and not appereth.
What may I do when my maister fereth,
    But, in the felde, with him to lyve and dye?
    For goode is the liff, ending faithfully.

                                      [after the Italian of Petrarch]

"Who so list to hounte I know where is an hynde"

Who so list to hounte I know where is an hynde;
    But as for me, helas, I may no more:
    The vayne travaill hath weried me so sore,
    I ame of theim that farthest cometh behinde;
Yet may I by no meanes my weried mynde
    Drawe from the Diere: but as she fleeth afore
    Faynting I folowe; I leve off therefore,
    Sithens in a nett I seke to hold the wynde.
Who list her hount I put him owte of dowbte,
    As well as I may spend his tyme in vain:
    And graven with Diamondes in letters plain
There is written her faier neck rounde abowte:
    'Noli me tangere for Cesars I ame,
    And wylde for to hold though I seme tame'.

                                        [after the Italian of Petrarch]

"Farewell, Love, and all thy lawes for ever"

Farewell, Love, and all thy lawes for ever;
 Thy bayted hookes shall tangill me no more;
 Senec and Plato call me from thy lore,
 To perfaict welth my wit for to endever.
In blynde errour when I did persever,
 Thy sherpe repulce that pricketh ay so sore
 Hath taught me to sett in tryfels no store
 And scape forth syns libertie is liefer.
Therefore, farewell; goo trouble yonger hertes
 And in me clayme no more authoritie;
 With idill yeuth goo use thy propertie
And theron spend thy many britill dertes:
 For hetherto though I have lost all my tyme,
 Me lusteth no lenger rotten boughes to clyme.

"My galy chargèd with forgetfulnes"

My galy chargèd with forgetfulnes
 Thorrough sharpe sees in wynter nyghtes doeth pas
 Twene Rock and Rock; and eke myn ennemy, Alas,
 That is my lorde, sterith with cruelnes;
And every houre a thought in readines,
 As thou that deth were light in suche a case;
 An endles wynd doeth tere the sayll a pace
 Of forcèd sightes and trusty ferefulnes.
A rayn of tearis, a clowde of derk disdain
 Hath done the wearied cordes great hinderaunce,
 Wrethèd with errour and eke with ignoraunce.
The starres be hid that led me to this pain;
 Drownèd is reason that s hould me confórt,
 And I remain dispering of the port.

      [after the Italian of Petrarch]

[4]

HENRY HOWARD, EARL OF SURREY

"The soote season, that bud and blome furth bringes"

The soote season, that bud and blome furth bringes,
With grene hath clad the hill and eke the vale;
The nightingale with fethers new she singes;
The turtle to her make hath tolde her tale.
Somer is come, for every spray nowe springes;
The hart hath hong his olde hed on the pale;
The buck in brake his winter cote he flinges;
The fishes flote with newe repairèd scale;
The adder all her sloughe awaye she slinges;
The swift swalow pursueth the flyes smale;
The busy bee her honye now she minges;
Winter is worne that was the flowers bale.
    And thus I see among these pleasant thinges
    Eche care decayes, and yet my sorow springes.

                            [after the Italian of Petrarch]

"Alas, so all thinges nowe doe holde their peace"

Alas, so all thinges nowe doe holde their peace,
Heaven and earth disturbèd in nothing;
The beastes, the ayer, the birdes their song doe cease;
The nightes chare the starres aboute dothe bring.
Calme is the sea, the waves worke lesse and lesse;
So am not I, whom love alas doth wring,
Bringing before my face the great encrease
Of my desires, whereat I wepe and syng
In joye and wo as in a doutfull ease.
For my swete thoughtes sometyme doe pleasure bring,
But by and by the cause of my disease
Geves me a pang that inwardly dothe sting,
    When that I thinke what griefe it is againe
    To live and lacke the thing should ridde my paine.

                            [after the Italian of Petrarch]

"Love that liveth and reigneth in my thought"

Love that liveth and reigneth in my thought,
That built his seat within my captive breast,
Clad in the arms wherein with me he fought,
Oft in my face he doth his banner rest.
She that me taught to love and suffer pain,
My doubtful hope and eke my hot desire
With shamefast cloak to shadow and refrain,
Her smiling grace converteth straight to ire;
And coward love then to the heart apace
Taketh his flight, whereas he lurks and plains
His purpose lost, and dare not show his face.
For my lord's guilt thus faultless bide I pains;
Yet from my lord shall not my foot remove,—
Sweet is his death that takes his end by love.

[after the Italian of Petrarch]

ANNE LOCKE

**from *A Meditation of a Penitent Sinner: Written in maner of a
Paraphrase upon the 51 Psalme of David***

Loe prostrate, Lorde, before thy face I lye
With sighes depe drawne depe sorrow to
    expresse,
O Lord of mercie, mercie do I crye:
Dryve me not from thy face in my distresse,
Thy face of mercie and of swete relefe
The face that fedes angels with onely sight,
The face of comfort in extremest grefe
Take not away the succour of thy sprite,
Thy holy sprite, which is myn onely stay,
The stay that when despeir assaileth me,
In faintest hope yet moveth me to pray,
To pray for mercy, and to pray to thee.
Lord, cast me not from presence of thy face,
Nor take from me the spirite of thy grace.

*Cast me not
away from thy
face and take not
thy holy spirit
from me.*

[6]

But render me my wonted joyes againe,
Which sinne hath reft, and planted in theyr
    place
Doubt of thy mercie ground of all my paine.
The tast that thy love whylome did embrace
My cheerfull soule, the signes that dyd assure
My felyng ghost of favour in thy sight,
Are fled from me, and wretched I endure
Senselesse of grace the absence of thy sprite.
Restore my joyes, and make me fele againe
The swete retorne of grace that I have lost,
That I may hope I pray not all in vayne.
With thy free sprite confirme my feble ghost,
To hold my faith from ruine and decay
With fast affiance and assured stay.

Restore to me the comforte of thy saving helpe, & stablishe me with thy free spirit.

GEORGE GASCOIGNE

"That self-same tongue which first did thee entreat"

That self-same tongue which first did thee entreat
To link thy liking with my lucky love,
That trusty tongue must now these words repeat,
I love thee still, my fancy cannot move.
That dreadless heart which durst attempt the thought
To win thy will with mine for to consent,
Maintains that vow which love in me first wrought,
I love thee still, and never shall repent.
That happy hand which hardly did touch
Thy tender body to my deep delight,
Shall serve with sword to prove my passion such
As loves thee still, much more than it can write.
    Thus love I still with tongue, hand, heart and all,
    And when I change, let vengeance on me fall.

EDMUND SPENSER

from *Amoretti*

8

More then most faire, full of the living fire,
    kindled above unto the maker neere:
    no eies but joyes, in which al powers conspire
    that to the world naught else be counted deare:
Thrugh your bright beames doth not the blindest guest
    shoot out his darts to base affections' wound?
    but Angels come to lead fraile mindes to rest
    in chast desires on heavenly beauty bound.
You frame my thoughts and fashion me within;
    you stop my toung, and teach my hart to speake;
    you calme the storme that passion did begin,
    strong thrugh your cause, but by your vertue weak.
Dark is the world, where your light shined never;
    well is he borne, that may behold you ever.

30

My love is lyke to yse, and I to fyre:
    how comes it then that this her cold so great
    is not dissolv'd through my so hot desyre,
    but harder growes the more I her intreat?
Or how comes it that my exceeding heat
    is not delayed by her hart frosen cold,
    but that I burne much more in boyling sweat,
    and feele my flames augmented manifold?
What more miraculous thing may be told
    that fire, which all thing melts, should harden yse:
    and yse which is congeald with sencelesse cold,
    should kindle fyre by wonderfull devyse?
Such is the powre of love in gentle mind
    that it can alter all the course of kynd.

37

What guyle is this, that those her golden tresses,
    she doth attyre under a net of gold,
    and with sly skill so cunningly them dresses,
    that which is gold or heare may scarse be told?
Is it that men's frayle eyes, which gaze too bold,
    she may entangle in that golden snare;
    and being caught, may craftily enfold
    theyr weaker harts, which are not wel aware?
Take heed therefore, myne eyes, how ye doe stare
    henceforth too rashly on that guilefull net,
    in which if ever ye entrapped are,
    out of her bands ye by no meanes shall get.
Fondnesse it were for any being free
    to covet fetters, though they golden bee.

68

Most glorious Lord of lyfe that on this day
    didst make thy triumph over death and sin,
    and having harrowd hell didst bring away
    captivity thence captive us to win:
This joyous day, deare Lord, with joy begin,
    and grant that we for whom thou diddest dye,
    being with thy deare blood clene washt from sin,
    may live for ever in felicity:
And that thy love we weighing worthily,
    may likewise love thee for the same againe;
    and for thy sake that all lyke deare didst buy,
    with love may one another entertayne.
So let us love, deare love, lyke as we ought:
    love is the lesson which the Lord us taught.

71

I joy to see how in your drawen work,
　　your selfe unto the Bee ye doe compare;
　　and me unto the Spyder that doth lurke
　　in close awayt to catch her unaware.
Right so your selfe were caught in cunning snare
　　of a deare foe, and thralled to his love;
　　in whose streight bands ye now captived are
　　so firmely, that ye never may remove.
But as your worke is woven all above
　　with woodbynd flowers and fragrant Eglantine,
　　so sweet your prison you in time shall prove,
　　with many deare delights bedecked fyne.
And all thensforth eternall peace shall see,
　　betweene the Spyder and the gentle Bee.

75

One day I wrote her name upon the strand,
　　but came the waves and washed it away:
　　agayne I wrote it with a second hand,
　　but came the tyde, and made my paynes his pray.
Vayne man, sayd she, that doest in vaine assay
　　a mortall thing so to immortalize,
　　for I my selve shall lyke to this decay,
　　and eek my name bee wyped out lykewize.
Not so, (quod I) let baser things devize
　　to dy in dust, but you shall live by fame:
　　my verse your vertues rare shall eternize,
　　and in the hevens wryte your glorious name:
Where, whenas death shall all the world subdew,
　　our love shall live, and later life renew.

78

Lackyng my love I go from place to place,
  lyke a young fawne that late hath lost the hynd;
  and seeke each where, where last I sawe her face,
  whose ymage yet I carry fresh in mynd.
I seeke the fields with her late footing synd,
  I seeke her bowre with her late presence deckt,
  yet nor in field nor bowre I her can fynd;
  yet field and bowre are full of her aspect.
But when myne eyes I thereunto direct,
  they ydly back returne to me agayne,
  and when I hope to see theyr trew object,
  I fynd my selfe but fed with fancies vayne.
Ceasse then, myne eyes, to seeke her selfe to see,
  and let my thoughts behold her selfe in mee.

79

Men call you fayre, and you doe credit it,
  for that your selfe ye dayly such doe see:
  but the trew fayre, that is the gentle wit
  and vertuous mind, is much more praysd of me.
For all the rest, how ever fayre it be,
  shall turne to nought and loose that glorious hew:
  but onely that is permanent and free
  from frayle corruption, that doth flesh ensew.
That is true beautie: that doth argue you
  to be divine and borne of heavenly seed,
  deriv'd from that fayre Spirit, from whom al true
  and perfect beauty did at first proceed.
He onely fayre, and what he fayre hath made:
  all other fayre lyke flowres untymely fade.

FULKE GREVILLE, LORD BROOKE

from *Cælica*

38

Cælica, I overnight was finely used,
Lodged in the midst of paradise, your heart;
Kind thoughts had charge I might not be refused,
Of every fruit and flower I had part.

But curious knowledge, blown with busy flame,
The sweetest fruits had in down shadows hidden,
And for it found mine eyes had seen the same,
I from my paradise was straight forbidden.

Where that cur, rumor, runs in every place,
Barking with care, begotten out of fear;
And glassy honor, tender of disgrace,
Stand seraphim to see I come not there;
    While that fine soil which all these joys did yield,
    By broken fence is proved a common field.

39

The *nurse-life* wheat, within his green husk growing,
Flatters our hope, and tickles our desire,
Nature's true riches in sweet beauties showing,
Which set all hearts, with labour's love, on fire.

No less fair is the wheat when golden ear
Shows unto hope the joys of near enjoying:
Fair and sweet is the bud, more sweet and fair
The rose, which proves that time is not destroying.

Cælica, your youth, the morning of delight,
Enamelled o'er with beauties white and red,
All sense and thoughts did to belief invite,
That love and glory there are brought to bed;
And your ripe years love none; he goes no higher,
    Turns all the spirits of man into desire.

In night when colours all to black are cast,
Distinction lost, or gone down with the light;
The eye a watch to inward senses plac'd,
Not seeing, yet still having power of sight,
Gives vain alarums to the inward sense,
Where fear stirr'd up with witty tyranny,
Confounds all powers, and thorough self-offence,
Doth forge and raise impossibility:
Such is in thick depriving darknesses,
Proper reflections of the error be,
And images of self-confusednesses,
Which hurt imaginations only see;
And from this nothing seen, tells news of devils,
Which but expressions be of inward evils.

SIR PHILIP SIDNEY

from *The Countess of Pembroke's Arcadia*

My true love hath my hart, and I have his,
By just exchange, one for the other giv'ne.
I holde his deare, and myne he cannot misse:
There never was a better bargaine driv'ne.

His hart in me, keepes me and him in one,
My hart in him, his thoughtes and senses guides:
He loves my hart, for once it was his owne:
I cherish his, because in me it bides.

His hart his wound receavèd from my sight:
My hart was wounded, with his wounded hart,
For as from me, on him his hurt did light,
So still me thought in me his hurt did smart:
    Both equall hurt, in this change sought our blisse:
    My true love hath my hart and I have his.

from *Astrophel and Stella*

1

Loving in truth, and faine in verse my love to show,
That she (deare she) might take some pleasure of my paine;
Pleasure might cause her reade, reading might make her know,
Knowledge might pitie winne, and pitie grace obtaine,
I sought fit words to paint the blackest face of woe,
Studying inventions fine her wits to entertaine;
Oft turning others' leaves, to see if thence would flow
Some fresh and fruitfull showers upon my sunne-burn'd braine.
  But words came halting forth, wanting Invention's stay;
Invention, Nature's child, fled step-dame Studie's blowes,
And others' feete still seem'd but strangers in my way.
Thus great with child to speake, and helplesse in my throwes,
    Biting my trewand pen, beating my selfe for spite,
    'Foole,' said my Muse to me, 'looke in thy heart and write.'

5

It is most true that eyes are form'd to serve
The inward light, and that the heavenly part
Ought to be king, from whose rules who do swerve,
    Rebels to Nature, strive for their owne smart.
    It is most true, what we call *Cupid's* dart,
An image is, which for our selves we carve,
And, fooles, adore in temple of our hart,
Till that good God make Church and Churchman starve.
    True, that true Beautie Vertue is indeed,
Whereof this Beautie can be but a shade
Which elements with mortall mixture breed:
True, that on earth we are but pilgrims made,
    And should in soule up to our countrey move:
    True, and yet true that I must *Stella* love.

31

With how sad steps, O Moone, thou climb'st the skies,
  How silently, and with how wanne a face;
  What, may it be that even in heav'nly place
That busie archer his sharpe arrowes tries?
Sure, if that long-with-*Love*-acquainted eyes
  Can judge of *Love*, thou feel'st a Lover's case;
  I reade it in thy lookes; thy languisht grace
To me that feele the like, thy state descries.
  Then ev'n of fellowship, O Moone, tell me
Is constant *Love* deem'd there but want of wit?
Are Beauties there as proud as here they be?
Do they above love to be lov'd, and yet
  Those Lovers scorne whom that *Love* doth possesse?
  Do they call *Vertue* there ungratefulnesse?

39

Come sleepe, O sleepe, the certaine knot of peace,
The baiting place of wit, the balme of woe,
The poore man's wealth, the prisoner's release,
Th'indifferent Judge betweene the high and low;
With shield of proofe shield me from out the prease
Of those fierce darts dispaire at me doth throw:
O make in me those civill warres to cease;
I will good tribute pay if thou do so.
  Take thou of me smooth pillowes, sweetest bed,
A chamber deafe to noise, and blind to light;
A rosie garland, and a wearie hed;
And if these things, as being thine by right,
  Move not thy heavy grace, thou shalt in me,
  Livelier then else-where, *Stella's* image see.

47

What, have I thus betrayed my libertie?
    Can those blacke beames such burning markes engrave
    In my free side? or am I borne a slave,
Whose necke becomes such yoke of tyranny?
Or want I sense to feele my miserie?
    Or sprite, disdaine of such disdaine to have,
    Who for long faith, tho dayly helpe I crave,
May get no almes but scorne of beggerie?
    Vertue awake; Beautie but beautie is:
I may, I must, I can, I will, I do
Leave following that, which it is gaine to misse.
Let her go. Soft, but here she comes. Go to,
    Unkind, I love you not: O me, that eye
    Doth make my heart give to my tongue the lie.

49

I on my horse, and *Love* on me doth trie
    Our horsmanships, while by strange worke I prove
    A horsman to my horse, a horse to *Love*;
And now man's wrongs in me, poore beast, descrie.
The raines wherewith my Rider doth me tie
    Are humbled thoughts, which bit of Reverence move,
    Curb'd in with feare, but with guilt bosse above
Of Hope, which makes it seeme faire to the eye.
    The Wand is Will; thou Fancie, Saddle art,
Girt fast by memorie, and while I spurre
My horse, he spurres with sharpe desire my hart:
He sits me fast, how ever I do sturre;
    And now hath made me to his hand so right,
    That in the Manage myselfe takes delight.

63

O Grammer rules, O now your vertues show;
    So children still reade you with awfull eyes,
    As my young Dove may, in your precepts wise,
Her graunt to me by her owne vertue know.
For late with heart most high, with eyes most low,
    I crav'd the thing which ever she denies:
    She, lightning *Love*, displaying *Venus'* skies,
Least once should not be heard, twise said, 'No, No.'
    Sing then, my Muse, now *Io Pean* sing;
    Heav'ns, envy not at my high triumphing,
But Grammer's force with sweet successe confirme;
    For Grammer sayes (O this, deare *Stella*, weighe,)
    For Grammer sayes (to Grammer who sayes nay?)
That in one speech two Negatives affirme.

71

Who will in fairest booke of Nature know
    How Vertue may best lodg'd in beautie be,
    Let him but learne of *Love* to reade in thee,
Stella, those faire lines which true goodnesse show.
There shall he find all vices' overthrow,
    Not by rude force, but sweetest soveraigntie
    Of reason, from whose light those night-birds flie,
That inward sunne in thine eyes shineth so:
    And not content to be Perfection's heire
Thy selfe, doest strive all minds that way to move,
Who marke in thee what is in thee most faire.
So while thy beautie drawes the heart to love,
    As fast thy Vertue bends that love to good:
    'But ah,' Desire still cries, 'give me some food.'

Stella, thinke not that I by verse seeke fame,
   Who seeke, who hope, who love, who live but thee;
   Thine eyes my pride, thy lips my history:
If thou praise not, all other praise is shame.
Nor so ambitious am I, as to frame
   A nest for my yong praise in Lawrell tree:
   In truth I sweare, I wish not there should be
Graved in mine Epitaph a Poet's name:
   Ne if I would, could I just title make,
That any laud to me thereof should grow,
Without my plumes from others' wings I take.
For nothing from my wit or will doth flow,
   Since all my words thy beauty doth endite,
   And love doth hold my hand, and makes me write.

from *Certaine Sonnets*

   Leave me, O Love, which reachest but to dust,
And thou, my mind, aspire to higher things:
Grow rich in that which never taketh rust:
What ever fades but fading pleasure brings.
   Draw in thy beames, and humble all thy might
To that sweet yoke, where lasting freedomes be,
Which breakes the clowdes and opens forth the light,
That doth both shine and give us sight to see.
   O take fast hold, let that light be thy guide,
In this small course which birth drawes out to death,
And thinke how evill becommeth him to slide,
Who seeketh heav'n, and comes of heav'nly breath.
   Then farewell world, thy uttermost I see:
   Eternall Love maintaine thy life in me.

SIR WALTER RALEGH

A vision upon This Conceipt of the Faery Queen

Methought I saw the grave where Laura lay,
Within that temple where the vestal flame
Was wont to burn; and passing by that way
To see that buried dust of living fame,
Whose tomb fair Love and fairer Virtue kept,
All suddenly I saw the Faery Queen:
At whose approach the soul of Petrarch wept;
And from thenceforth those Graces were not seen,
For they this Queen attended; in whose stead
Oblivion laid him down on Laura's hearse.
Hereat the hardest stones were seen to bleed,
And groans of buried ghosts the heavens did pierce,
    Where Homer's spright did tremble all for grief,
    And cursed the access of that celestial thief.

Sir Walter Ralegh to His Son

Three things there be that prosper up apace
And flourish, whilst they grow asunder far;
But on a day, they meet all in one place,
And when they meet they one another mar:
And they be these—the wood, the weed, the wag.
The wood is that which makes the gallow tree;
The weed is that which strings the hangman's bag;
The wag, my pretty knave, betokeneth thee.
Mark well, dear boy, whilst these assemble not,
Green springs the tree, hemp grows, the wag is wild;
But when they meet, it makes the timber rot,
It frets the halter, and it chokes the child.
    Then bless thee, and beware, and let us pray
    We part not with thee at this meeting day.

GEORGE CHAPMAN

from *A Coronet for his Mistress Philosophy*

I

Muses that sing Love's sensual empery,
And lovers kindling your enraged fires
At Cupid's bonfires burning in the eye,
Blown with the empty breath of vain desires,—
You that prefer the painted cabinet
Before the wealthy jewels it doth store ye,
That all your joys in dying figures set,
And stain the living substance of your glory;
Abjure those joys, abhor their memory,
And let my Love the honoured subject be
Of love, and honour's complete history;
Your eyes were never yet let in to see
The majesty and riches of the mind,
But dwell in darkness; for your god is blind.

HENRY CONSTABLE

from *Diana* (1594 edition)

Needs must I leave and yet needs must I love
In vayne my witt doth paynt in verse my woe
Disdaine in thee dispaire in me doth showe
How by my witte I doe my follie prove

All this my heart from love can never move
Love is not in my heart, no Lady no,
My hearte is love it selfe; till I forgoe
My hearte, I never can my love remove.

How shall I then leave love? I do entend
Not to crave grace but yet to wish it still
Not to prayse thee, but beautie to commend
And so by beauties prayse, prayse thee I will
  For as my heart is love, love not in me
  So beautie thou beautie is not in thee.

MARK ALEXANDER BOYD

Sonet

Fra banc to banc, fra wod to wod, I rin
    Owrhailit with my feble fantasie,
    Lyc til a leif that fallis from a trie
    Or til a reid owrblawin with the win'.
Twa gods gyds me: the ane of tham is blin',
    Ye, and a bairn brocht up in vanitie;
    The nixt a wyf ingenrit of the se,
    And lichter nor a dauphin with hir fin.
Unhappie is the man for evirmaire
    That teils the sand and sawis in the aire,
    Bot twyse unhappier is he, I lairn,
That feidis in his hairt a mad desyre,
    And follows on a woman throu the fyre,
    Led be a blind and teichit be a bairn.

SAMUEL DANIEL

from *To Delia*

34
Looke, *Delia*, how wee steeme the half-blowne Rose,
    The image of thy blush, and Sommer's honour,
    Whilst in her tender greene shee doth inclose
    The pure sweet beauty Time bestowes upon her:
No sooner spreades her glory in the ayre,
    But straight her ful-blowne pride is in declining;
    Shee then is scorn'd, that late adorn'd the fayre:
    So clowdes thy beautie, after fairest shining.
No Aprill can revive thy withred flowers,
    Whose blooming grace adornes thy glory now:
    Swift speedy Time, feathred with flying howers,
    Dissolves the beautie of the fairest brow.
O let not then such riches waste in vaine;
But love whist thou maist be lov'd againe.

49

Care-charmer Sleepe, sonne of the sable Night,
    Brother to death, in silent darknes borne;
    Relieve my languish, and restore the light,
    With darke forgetting of my care's returne:
And let the day be time enough to mourne
    The shipwrack of my ill-adventred youth:
    Let waking eyes suffice to waile their scorne,
    Without the torment of the night's untruth.
Cease dreames, th'imag'ry of our day desires,
    To modell forth the passions of the morrow:
    Never let rysing Sunne approve you lyers,
    To adde more griefe to agravate my sorrow.
Still let me sleepe, imbracing clowdes in vaine,
And never wake to feele the daye's disdayne.

50

Let others sing of Knights and Palladines
    In aged accents and untimely words,
    Paint shadowes in imaginarie lines,
    Which wel the reach of their high wits records:
But I must sing of thee and those faire eyes;
    Autentique shall my verse in time to come,
    When yet th'unborne shall say, 'Loe, where she lyes,
    Whose beauty made him speak that else was dombe.'
These are the Arkes, the Trophies I erect,
    That fortifie thy name against old age;
    And these thy sacred vertues must protect
    Against the darke, and Time's consuming rage.
Though th'error of my youth they shall discover,
Suffice, they shew I liv'd and was thy lover.

MICHAEL DRAYTON

from *Idea in Sixtie Three Sonnets*

6

How many paltry, foolish, painted things,
That now in Coaches trouble ev'ry Street,
Shall be forgotten, whom no Poet sings,
Ere they be well wrap'd in their winding Sheet!
Where I to thee Eternitie shall give,
When nothing else remayneth of these dayes,
And Queenes hereafter shall be glad to live
Upon the Almes of thy superfluous prayse:
Virgins and Matrons reading these my Rimes,
Shall be so much delighted with thy story,
That they shall grieve they liv'd not in these Times,
To have seene thee, their Sexe's onely glory:
    So shalt thou flye above the vulgar Throng,
    Still to survive in my immortal Song.

61

Since ther's no helpe, Come let us kisse and part,
Nay, I have done: You get no more of Me,
And I am glad, yea glad with all my heart,
That thus so cleanly I my Selfe can free;
Shake hands for ever, Cancell all our Vowes,
And when We meet at any time againe,
Be it not seene in either of our Browes,
That we one jot of former Love reteyne:
Now at the last gaspe of Love's latest Breath,
When his Pulse fayling, Passion speechlesse lies,
When Faith is kneeling by his bed of Death,
And Innocence is closing up his eyes,
    Now if thou would'st, when all have given him over,
    From Death to Life thou might'st him yet recover.

JOHN DAVIES OF HEREFORD

*The author loving these homely meats specially, viz.: cream,
pancakes, buttered pippin-pies (laugh, good people) and tobacco;
writ to that worthy and virtuous gentlewoman, whom he calleth
mistress, as followeth*

If there were, oh! an Hellespont of cream
Between us, milk-white mistress, I would swim
To you, to show to both my love's extreme,
Leander-like,—yea! dive from brim to brim.
But met I with a buttered pippin-pie
Floating upon 't, that would I make my boat
To waft me to you without jeopardy,
Though sea-sick I might be while it did float.
Yet if a storm should rise, by night or day,
Of sugar-snows and hail of caraways,
Then, if I found a pancake in my way,
It like a plank should bring me to your kays;
    Which having found, if they tobacco kept,
    The smoke should dry me well before I slept.

CHARLES BEST

Of the Moon

Look how the pale queen of the silent night
    Doth cause the Ocean to attend upon her,
And he, as long as she is in his sight,
    With his full tide is ready her to honour;
But when the silver waggon of the Moon
    Is mounted up so high he cannot follow,
The sea calls home his crystal waves to moan,
    And with low ebb doth manifest his sorrow.
So you, that are the sovereign of my heart,
    Have all my joys attending on your will,
My joys low-ebbing when you do depart—
    When you return, their tide my heart doth fill:
        So as you come, and as you do depart,
        Joys ebb and flow within my tender heart.

WILLIAM SHAKESPEARE

from *Love's Labour's Lost* [Act IV, Scene III]

Did not the heavenly rhetoric of thine eye,
'Gainst whom the world cannot hold argument,
Persuade my heart to this false perjury?
Vows for thee broke deserve not punishment.
A woman I forswore, but I will prove,
Thou being a goddess, I forswore not thee.
My vow was earthly, thou a heavenly love;
Thy grace being gained cures all disgrace in me.
Vows are but breath, and breath a vapor is.
Then thou, fair sun, which on my earth doth shine,
Exhalest this vapor-vow; in thee it is.
If broken then, it is no fault of mine.
If by me broke, what fool is not so wise
To lose an oath to win a paradise?

from *Romeo and Juliet* [Act I, Scene V]

ROMEO. If I profane with my unworthiest hand
   This holy shrine, the gentle fine is this,
   My lips, two blushing pilgrims, ready stand
   To smooth that rough touch with a tender kiss.

JULIET. Good pilgrim, you do wrong your hand too much,
   Which mannerly devotion shows in this;
   For saints have hands that pilgrims' hands do touch,
   And palm to palm is holy palmers' kiss.

ROMEO: Have not saints lips, and holy palmers too?
JULIET. Aye, pilgrim, lips that they must use in prayer.
ROMEO. Oh then, dear saint, let lips do what hands do.
   Then pray. Grant thou, lest faith turn to despair.

JULIET. Saints do not move, though grant for prayers' sake.
ROMEO. Then move not while my prayer's effect I take.

from *Sonnets*

3

Look in thy glass, and tell the face thou viewest
Now is the time that face should form another,
Whose fresh repair if now thou not renewest,
Thou dost beguile the world, unbless some mother.
For where is she so fair whose uneared womb
Disdains the tillage of thy husbandry?
Or who is he so fond will be the tomb
Of his self-love, to stop posterity?
Thou art thy mother's glass, and she in thee
Calls back the lovely April of her prime;
So thou through windows of thine age shalt see,
Despite of wrinkles, this thy golden time.

    But if thou live rememb'red not to be,
    Die single, and thine image dies with thee.

18

Shall I compare thee to a summer's day?
Thou art more lovely and more temperate.
Rough winds do shake the darling buds of May,
And summer's lease hath all too short a date.
Sometime too hot the eye of heaven shines,
And often is his gold complexion dimmed;
And every fair from fair sometime declines,
By chance, or nature's changing course, untrimmed:
But thy eternal summer shall not fade
Nor lose possession of that fair thou ow'st,
Nor shall Death brag thou wand'rest in his shade
When in eternal lines to time thou grow'st.

    So long as men can breathe or eyes can see,
    So long lives this, and this gives life to thee.

20

A woman's face, with Nature's own hand painted,
Hast thou, the master-mistress of my passion;
A woman's gentle heart, but not acquainted
With shifting change, as is false women's fashion;
An eye more bright than theirs, less false in rolling,
Gilding the object whereupon it gazeth;
A man in hue all hues in his controlling,
Which steals men's eyes and women's souls amazeth.
And for a woman wert thou first created,
Till Nature as she wrought thee fell a-doting,
And by addition me of thee defeated
By adding one thing to my purpose nothing.
    But since she pricked thee out for women's pleasure,
    Mine be thy love, and thy love's use their treasure.

27

Weary with toil, I haste me to my bed,
The dear repose for limbs with travel tired,
But then begins a journey in my head
To work my mind when body's work's expired;
For then my thoughts, from far where I abide,
Intend a zealous pilgrimage to thee,
And keep my drooping eyelids open wide,
Looking on darkness which the blind do see;
Save that my soul's imaginary sight
Presents thy shadow to my sightless view,
Which, like a jewel hung in ghastly night,
Makes black night beauteous and her old face new.
    Lo, thus, by day my limbs, by night my mind,
    For thee and for myself no quiet find.

29

When, in disgrace with Fortune and men's eyes,
I all alone beweep my outcast state,
And trouble deaf heaven with my bootless cries,
And look upon myself and curse my fate,
Wishing me like to one more rich in hope,
Featured like him, like him with friends possessed,
Desiring this man's art, and that man's scope,
With what I most enjoy contented least;
Yet in these thoughts myself almost despising,
Haply I think on thee, and then my state,
Like to the lark at break of day arising
From sullen earth, sings hymns at heaven's gate;
    For thy sweet love rememb'red such wealth brings
    That then I scorn to change my state with kings.

53

What is your substance, whereof are you made,
That millions of strange shadows on you tend?
Since every one hath, every one, one shade,
And you, but one, can every shadow lend.
Describe Adonis, and the counterfeit
Is poorly imitated after you.
On Helen's cheek all art of beauty set,
And you in Grecian tires are painted new.
Speak of the spring and foison of the year:
The one doth shadow of your beauty show,
The other as your bounty doth appear,
And you in ever blessèd shape we know.
    In all external grace you have some part,
    But you like none, none you, for constant heart.

55

Not marble nor the gilded monuments
Of princes shall outlive this pow'rful rime,
But you shall shine more bright in these contents
Than unswept stone, besmeared with sluttish time.
When wasteful war shall statues overturn,
And broils root out the work of masonry,
Nor Mars his sword nor war's quick fore shall burn
The living record of your memory.
'Gainst death and all oblivious enmity
Shall you pace forth; your praise shall still find room
Even in the eyes of all posterity
That wear this world out to the ending doom.
    So, till the judgment that yourself arise,
      You live in this, and dwell in lovers' eyes.

60

Like as the waves make towards the pebbled shore,
So do our minutes hasten to their end;
Each changing place with that which goes before,
In sequent toil all forwards do contend.
Nativity, once in the main of light,
Crawls to maturity, wherewith being crowned,
Crooked eclipses 'gainst his glory fight,
And Time that gave doth now his gift confound.
Time doth transfix the flourish set on youth
And delves the parallels in beauty's brow,
Feeds on the rarities of nature's truth,
And nothing stands but for his scythe to mow:
    And yet to times in hope my verse shall stand,
      Praising thy worth, despite his cruel hand.

65

Since brass, nor stone, nor earth, nor boundless sea,
But sad mortality o'ersways their power,
How with this rage shall beauty hold a plea,
Whose action is no stronger than a flower?
O, how shall summer's honey breath hold out
Against the wrackful siege of batt'ring days,
When rocks impregnable are not so stout,
Nor gates of steel so strong but Time decays?
O fearful meditation: where, alack,
Shall Time's best jewel from Time's chest lie hid?
Or what strong hand can hold his swift foot back,
Or who his spoil of beauty can forbid?
    O, none, unless this miracle have might,
    That in black ink my love may still shine bright.

71

No longer mourn for me when I am dead
Than you shall hear the surly sullen bell
Give warning to the world that I am fled
From this vile world, with vilest worms to dwell.
Nay, if you read this line, remember not
The hand that writ it, for I love you so
That I in your sweet thoughts would be forgot
If thinking on me then should make you woe.
O, if, I say, you look upon this verse
When I, perhaps, compounded am with clay,
Do not so much as my poor name rehearse,
But let your love even with my life decay,
    Lest the wise world should look into your moan
    And mock you with me after I am gone.

73

That time of year thou mayst in me behold
When yellow leaves, or none, or few, do hang
Upon those boughs which shake against the cold,
Bare ruined choirs where late the sweet birds sang.
In me thou seest the twilight of such day
As after sunset fadeth in the west,
Which by and by black night doth take away,
Death's second self that seals up all in rest.
In me thou seest the glowing of such fire
That on the ashes of his youth doth lie,
As the deathbed whereon it must expire,
Consumed with that which it was nourished by.
    This thou perceiv'st, which makes thy love more strong,
    To love that well which thou must leave ere long.

94

They that have pow'r to hurt and will do none,
That do not do the thing they most do show,
Who, moving others, are themselves as stone,
Unmovèd, cold, and to temptation slow;
They rightly do inherit heaven's graces
And husband nature's riches from expense;
They are the lords and owners of their faces,
Others but stewards of their excellence.
The summer's flow'r is to the summer sweet,
Though to itself it only live and die;
But if that flow'r with base infection meet,
The basest weed outbraves his dignity:
    For sweetest things turn sourest by their deeds;
    Lilies that fester smell far worse than weeds.

106

When in the chronicle of wasted time
I see descriptions of the fairest wights,
And beauty making beautiful old rime
In praise of ladies dead and lovely knights;
Then, in the blazon of sweet beauty's best,
Of hand, of foot, of lip, of eye, of brow,
I see their antique pen would have expressed
Even such a beauty as you master now.
So all their praises are but prophecies,
Of this our time, all you prefiguring;
And, for they looked but with divining eyes,
They had not skill enough your worth to sing:
    For we, which now behold these present days,
    Have eyes to wonder, but lack tongues to praise.

116

Let me not to the marriage of true minds
Admit impediments; love is not love
Which alters when it alteration finds
Or bends with the remover to remove.
O, no, it is an ever-fixèd mark
That looks on tempests and is never shaken;
It is the star to every wand'ring bark,
Whose worth's unknown, although his height be taken.
Love's not Time's fool, though rosy lips and cheeks
Within his bending sickle's compass come;
Love alters not with his brief hours and weeks,
But bears it out even to the edge of doom.
    If this be error, and upon me proved,
    I never writ, nor no man ever loved.

127

In the old age black was not counted fair,
Or, if it were, it bore not beauty's name;
But now is black beauty's successive heir,
And beauty slandered with a bastard shame;
For since each hand hath put on nature's power,
Fairing the foul with art's false borrowed face,
Sweet beauty hath no name, no holy bower,
But is profaned, if not lives in disgrace.
Therefore my mistress' brows are raven black,
Her eyes so suited, and they mourners seem
At such who, not born fair, no beauty lack,
Sland'ring creation with a false esteem:
    Yet so they mourn, becoming of their woe,
    That every tongue says beauty should look so.

128

How oft, when thou, my music, music play'st
Upon that blessèd wood whose motion sounds
With thy sweet fingers when thou gently sway'st
The wiry concord that mine ear confounds,
Do I envy those jacks that nimble leap
To kiss the tender inward of thy hand,
Whilst my poor lips, which should that harvest reap,
At the wood's boldness by thee blushing stand.
To be so tickled they would change their state
And situation with those dancing chips
O'er whom thy fingers walk with gentle gait,
Making dead wood more blest than living lips.
    Since saucy jacks so happy are in this,
    Give them thy fingers, me thy lips to kiss.

129

Th' expense of spirit in a waste of shame
Is lust in action; and, till action, lust
Is perjured, murd'rous, bloody, full of blame,
Savage, extreme, rude, cruel, not to trust;
Enjoyed no sooner but despisèd straight;
Past reason hunted, and no sooner had,
Past reason hated as a swallowed bait
On purpose laid to make the taker mad:
Mad in pursuit, and in possession so;
Had, having, and in quest to have, extreme;
A bliss in proof, and proved, a very woe;
Before, a joy proposed; behind, a dream.
    All this the world well knows; yet none knows well
    To shun the heaven that leads men to this hell.

130

My mistress' eyes are nothing like the sun;
Coral is far more red than her lips' red;
If snow be white, why then her breasts are dun;
If hairs be wires, black wires grow on her head.
I have seen roses damasked, red and white,
But no such roses see I in her cheeks;
And in some perfumes is there more delight
Than in the breath that from my mistress reeks.
I love to hear her speak; yet well I know
That music hath a far more pleasing sound:
I grant I never saw a goddess go;
My mistress, when she walks, treads on the ground.
    And yet, by heaven, I think my love as rare
    As any she belied with false compare.

138

When my love swears that she is made of truth
I do believe her, though I know she lies,
That she might think me some untutored youth,
Unlearnèd in the world's false subtilties.
Thus vainly thinking that she thinks me young,
Although she knows my days are past the best,
Simply I credit her false-speaking tongue;
On both sides thus is simple truth suppressed.
But wherefore says she not she is unjust?
And wherefore say not I that I am old?
O, love's best habit is in seeming trust,
And age in love loves not to have years told.
    Therefore I lie with her and she with me,
    And in our faults by lies we flattered be.

141

In faith, I do not love thee with mine eyes,
For they in thee a thousand errors note;
But 'tis my heart that loves what they despise,
Who in despite of view is pleased to dote.
Nor are mine ears with thy tongue's tune delighted,
Nor tender feeling to base touches prone,
Nor taste, nor smell, desire to be invited
To any sensual feast with thee alone;
But my five wits nor my five senses can
Dissuade one foolish heart from serving thee,
Who leaves unswayed the likeness of a man,
Thy proud heart's slave and vassal wretch to be:
    Only my plague thus far I count my gain,
    That she that makes me sin awards me pain.

Poor soul, the center of my sinful earth,
[Pressed by] these rebel pow'rs that thee array,
Why dost thou pine within and suffer dearth,
Painting thy outward walls so costly gay?
Why so large cost, having so short a lease,
Dost thou upon thy fading mansion spend?
Shall worms, inheritors of this excess,
Eat up thy charge? Is this thy body's end?
Then, soul, live thou upon thy servant's loss,
And let that pine to aggravate thy store;
Buy terms divine in selling hours of dross;
Within be fed, without be rich no more:
    So shalt thou feed on Death, that feeds on men,
    And Death once dead, there's no more dying then.

151

Love is too young to know what conscience is;
Yet who knows not conscience is born of love?
Then, gentle cheater, urge not my amiss,
Lest guilty of my faults thy sweet self prove.
For, thou betraying me, I do betray
My nobler part to my gross body's treason;
My soul doth tell my body that he may
Triumph in love; flesh stays no farther reason,
But, rising at thy name, doth point out thee
As his triumphant prize. Proud of this pride,
He is contented thy poor drudge to be,
To stand in thy affairs, fall by thy side.
    No want of conscience hold it that I call
    Her 'love' for whose dear love I rise and fall.

SIR JOHN DAVIES

"If you would know the love which I you bear"

If you would know the love which I you bear,
Compare it to the Ring which your fair hand
Shall make more precious when you shall it wear:
So my love's nature you shall understand.
Is it of metal pure? so you shall prove
My love, which ne'er disloyal thought did stain.
Hath it no end? so endless is my love,
Unless you it destroy with your disdain.
Doth it the purer wax the more 'tis tried?
So doth my love: yet herein they dissent,
That whereas gold, the more 'tis purified,
By waxing less doth show some part is spent,
My love doth wax more pure by your more trying,
And yet increaseth in the purifying.

JOHN DONNE

La Corona

I
Deign at my hands this crown of prayer and praise,
Weaved in my low devout melancholy,
Thou which of good, hast, yea art treasury,
All changing unchanged Ancient of days,
But do not, with a vile crown of frail bays,
Reward my muse's white sincerity,
But what thy thorny crown gained, that give me,
A crown of glory, which doth flower always;
The ends crown our works, but thou crown'st our ends,
For, at our end begins our endless rest,
This first last end, now zealously possessed,
With a strong sober thirst, my soul attends.
'Tis time that heart and voice be lifted high,
Salvation to all that will is nigh.

2 ANNUNCIATION

Salvation to all that will is nigh,
That all, which always is all everywhere,
Which cannot sin, and yet all sins must bear,
Which cannot die, yet cannot choose but die,
Lo, faithful Virgin, yields himself to lie
In prison, in thy womb; and though he there
Can take no sin, nor thou give, yet he 'will wear
Taken from thence, flesh, which death's force may try.
Ere by the spheres time was created, thou
Wast in his mind, who is thy son, and brother,
Whom thou conceiv'st, conceived; yea thou art now
Thy maker's maker, and thy father's mother,
Thou' hast light in dark; and shutt'st in little room,
Immensity cloistered in thy dear womb.

3 NATIVITY

Immensity cloistered in thy dear womb,
Now leaves his well-beloved imprisonment,
There he hath made himself to his intent
Weak enough, now into our world to come;
But oh, for thee, for him, hath th'inn no room?
Yet lay him in this stall, and from the orient,
Stars, and wisemen will travel to prevent
Th' effect of Herod's jealous general doom.
See'st thou, my soul, with thy faith's eyes, how he
Which fills all place, yet none holds him, doth lie?
Was not his pity towards thee wondrous high,
That would have need to be pitied by thee?
Kiss him, and with him into Egypt go,
With his kind mother, who partakes thy woe.

4 TEMPLE

With his kind mother who partakes thy woe,
Joseph turn back; see where your child doth sit,
Blowing, yea blowing out those sparks of wit,
Which himself on the Doctors did bestow;
The Word but lately could not speak, and lo
It suddenly speaks wonders, whence comes it,
That all which was, and all which should be writ,
A shallow seeming child, should deeply know?
His godhead was not soul to his manhood,
Nor had time mellowed him to this ripeness,
But as for one which hath a long task, 'tis good,
With the sun to begin his business,
He in his age's morning thus began
By miracles exceeding power of man.

5 CRUCIFYING

By miracles exceeding power of man,
He faith in some, envy in some begat,
For, what weak spirits admire, ambitious hate;
In both affections many to him ran,
But oh! the worst are most, they will and can,
Alas, and do, unto the immaculate,
Whose creature Fate is, now prescribe a fate,
Measuring self-life's infinity to a span,
Nay to an inch. Lo, where condemned he
Bears his own cross, with pain, yet by and by
When it bears him, he must bear more and die.
Now thou are lifted up, draw me to thee,
And at thy death giving such liberal dole,
Moist, with one drop of thy blood, my dry soul.

6 RESURRECTION

Moist with one drop of thy blood, my dry soul
Shall (though she now be in extreme degree
Too stony hard, and yet too fleshly,) be
Freed by that drop, from being starved, hard, or foul,
And life, by this death abled, shall control
Death, whom thy death slew; nor shall to me
Fear of first or last death, bring misery,
If in thy little book my name thou enrol,
Flesh in that long sleep is not putrefied,
But made that there, of which, and for which 'twas;
Nor can by other means be glorified.
May then sin's sleep, and death's soon from me pass,
That waked from both, I again risen may
Salute the last, and everlasting day.

7 ASCENSION

Salute the last and everlasting day,
Joy at the uprising of this sun, and son,
Ye whose just tears, or tribulation
Have purely washed, or burnt your drossy clay;
Behold the highest, parting hence away,
Lightens the dark clouds, which he treads upon,
Nor doth he by ascending, show alone,
But first he, and he first enters the way.
O strong ram, which hast battered heaven for me,
Mild lamb, which with thy blood, hast marked the path;
Bright torch, which shin'st, that I the way may see,
Oh, with thine own blood quench thine own just wrath,
And if thy holy Spirit, my Muse did raise,
Deign at my hands this crown of prayer and praise.

from *Holy Sonnets*

1

Thou hast made me, and shall thy work decay?
Repair me now, for now mine end doth haste,
I run to death, and death meets me as fast,
And all my pleasures are like yesterday,
I dare not move my dim eyes any way,
Despair behind, and death before doth cast
Such terror, and my feeble flesh doth waste
By sin in it, which it towards hell doth weigh;
Only thou art above, and when towards thee
By thy leave I can look, I rise again;
But our old subtle foe so tempteth me,
That not one hour I can myself sustain;
Thy Grace may wing me to prevent his art,
And thou like adamant draw mine iron heart.

6

This is my play's last scene, here heavens appoint
My pilgrimage's last mile; and my race
Idly, yet quickly run, hath this last pace,
My span's last inch, my minute's latest point,
And gluttonous death, will instantly unjoint
My body, and soul, and I shall sleep a space,
But my'ever-waking part shall see that face,
Whose fear already shakes my every joint:
Then, as my soul, to heaven her first seat, takes flight,
And earth-born body, in the earth shall dwell,
So, fall my sins, that all may have their right,
To where they are bred, and would press me, to hell.
Impute me righteous, thus purged of evil,
For thus I leave the world, the flesh, and devil.

7

At the round earth's imagined corners, blow
Your trumpets, angels, and arise, arise
From death, you numberless infinities
Of souls, and to your scattered bodies go,
All whom the flood did, and fire shall o'erthrow,
All whom war, dearth, age, agues, tyrannies,
Despair, law, chance, hath slain, and you whose eyes,
Shall behold God, and never taste death's woe.
But let them sleep, Lord, and me mourn a space,
For, if above all these, my sins abound,
'Tis late to ask abundance of thy grace,
When we are there; here on this lowly ground,
Teach me how to repent; for that's as good
As if thou hadst sealed my pardon, with thy blood.

10

Death be not proud, though some have callèd thee
Mighty and dreadful, for, thou art not so,
For, those, whom thou think'st, thou dost overthrow,
Die not, poor death, nor yet canst thou kill me;
From rest and sleep, which but thy pictures be,
Much pleasure, then from thee, much more must flow,
And soonest our best men with thee do go,
Rest of their bones, and soul's delivery.
Thou art slave to fate, chance, kings, and desperate men,
And dost with poison, war, and sickness dwell,
And poppy, or charms can make us sleep as well,
And better than thy stroke; why swell'st thou then?
One short sleep past, we wake eternally,
And death shall be no more, Death thou shalt die.

14

Batter my heart, three-personed God; for, you
As yet but knock, breathe, shine, and seek to mend;
That I may rise, and stand, o'erthrow me, and bend
Your force, to break, blow, burn, and make me new.
I, like an usurped town, to another due,
Labour to admit you, but oh, to no end,
Reason your viceroy in me, me should defend,
But is captived, and proves weak or untrue,
Yet dearly'I love you, and would be loved fain,
But am betrothed unto your enemy,
Divorce me, untie, or break that knot again,
Take me to you, imprison me, for I
Except you enthral me, never shall be free,
Nor ever chaste, except you ravish me.

19

Oh, to vex me, contraries meet in one:
Inconstancy unnaturally hath begot
A constant habit; that when I would not
I change in vows, and in devotion.
As humorous is my contrition
As my profane love, and as soon forgot:
As riddlingly distempered, cold and hot,
As praying, as mute; as infinite, as none.
I durst not view heaven yesterday; and today
In prayers, and flattering speeches I court God:
Tomorrow I quake with true fear of his rod.
So my devout fits come and go away
Like a fantastic ague: save that here
Those are my best days, when I shake with fear.

Sonnet. The Token

Send me some token, that my hope may live,
    Or that my easeless thoughts may sleep and rest;
Send me some honey to make sweet my hive,
    That in my passions I may hope the best.
I beg no riband wrought with thine own hands,
    To knit our loves in the fantastic strain
Of new-touched youth; nor ring to show the stands
    Of our affection, that as that's round and plain,
So should our loves meet in simplicity;
    No, nor the corals which thy wrist enfold,
Laced up together in congruity,
    To show our thoughts should rest in the same hold;
No, nor thy picture, though most gracious,
    And most desired, because best like the best;
Nor witty lines, which are most copious,
    Within the writings which thou hast addressed.

Send me nor this, nor that, to increase my store,
But swear thou think'st I love thee, and no more.

BEN JONSON

A Sonnet to the Noble Lady, the Lady Mary Wroth

I that have been a lover, and could shew it,
    Though not in these, in rithmes not wholly dumb,
    Since I exscribe your sonnets, am become
    A better lover, and much better poet.
Nor is my Muse or I ashamed to owe it
    To those true numerous graces; whereof some
    But charm the senses, others overcome
    Both brains and hearts; and mine now best do know it:
For in your verse all Cupid's armoury,
    His flames, his shafts, his quiver, and his bow,
    His very eyes are yours to overthrow.
But then his mother's sweets you so apply,
    Her joys, her smiles, her loves, as readers take
    For Venus' ceston every line you make.

LORD HERBERT OF CHERBURY

Sonnet to Black It Self

Thou Black, wherein all colours are compos'd,
And unto which they all at last return,
Thou colour of the Sun where it doth burn,
And shadow, where it cools, in thee is clos'd
Whatever nature can or hath dispos'd
In any other hue: from thee do rise
Those tempers and complexions, which, disclos'd
As parts of thee, do work as mysteries
Of that thy hidden power: when thou dost reign,
The characters of fate shine in the Skies,
And tell us what the Heavens do ordain,
But when Earth's common light shines to our eyes,
Thou so retirest thyself, that thy disdain
All revelation unto Man denies.

WILLIAM DRUMMOND OF HAWTHORNDEN

"I know that all beneath the moon decays"

I know that all beneath the moon decays,
And what by mortals in this world is brought,
In Time's great periods shall return to nought;
That fairest states have fatal nights and days;
I know how all the Muse's heavenly lays,
With toil of spright which are so dearly bought,
As idle sounds of few or none are sought,
And that nought lighter is than airy praise.
I know frail beauty like the purple flower,
To which one morn oft birth and death affords;
That love a jarring is of minds' accords,
Where sense and will invassal reason's power:
Know what I list, this all can not me move,
But that, O me! I both must write and love.

"Sleep, Silence' child, sweet father of soft rest"

Sleep, Silence' child, sweet father of soft rest,
Prince whose approach peace to all mortals brings,
Indifferent host to shepherds and to kings,
Sole comforter of minds with grief opprest;
Lo, by thy charming-rod all breathing things
Lie slumbering, with forgetfulness possest,
And yet o'er me to spread thy drowsy wings
Thou spares, alas! who cannot be thy guest.
Since I am thine, O come, but with that face
To inward light which thou art wont to show;
With feigned solace each a true-felt woe;
Or if, deaf god, thou do deny that grace,
Come as thou wilt, and what thou wilt bequeath,—
I long to kiss the image of my death.

LADY MARY WROTH

from *A crowne of Sonetts dedicated to Love*

In this strang labourinth how shall I turne?
    wayes are on all sids while the way I miss:
    if to the right hand, ther, in love I burne;
    lett mee goe forward, therin danger is;

If to the left, suspition hinders bliss,
    lett mee turne back, shame cries I ought returne
    nor fainte though crosses with my fortunes kiss;
    stand still is harder, allthough sure to mourne;

Thus lett mee take the right, or left hand way;
    goe forward, or stand still, or back retire;
    I must thes doubts indure with out allay
    or help, butt traveile find for my best hire;

yett that which most my troubled sence doth move
is to leave all, and take the thread of love,

Is to leave all, and take the thread of love
    which line straite leads unto the soules content
    wher choyce delights with pleasures wings doe move,
    and idle phant'sie never roome had lent,

When chaste thoughts guide us then owr minds ar bent
    to take that good which ills from us remove,
    light of true love, brings fruite which none repent
    butt constant lovers seeke, and wish to prove;

Love is the shining starr of blessings light;
    the fervent fire of zeale, the roote of peace,
    that lasting lampe fed with the oyle of right;
    Image of fayth, and wombe for joyes increase.

Love is true vertu, and his ends delight,
his flames ar joyes, his bands true lovers might.

ROBERT HERRICK

To his mistress objecting to him neither toying nor talking

You say I love not, 'cause I do not play
    Still with your curls, and kiss the time away.
    You blame me, too, because I can't devise
    Some sport to please those babies in your eyes;—
By Love's religion, I must here confess it,
    The most I love, when I the least express it.
    Small griefs find tongues; full casks are ever found
    To give, if any, yet but little sound.
Deep waters noiseless are; and this we know,
    That chiding streams betray small depth below.
    So when love speechless is, she doth express
    A depth in love, and that depth bottomless.
Now, since my love is tongueless, know me such,
    Who speak but little, 'cause I love so much.

GEORGE HERBERT

Two Sonnets sent to his Mother, New-year 1609/10

My God, where is that ancient heat towards thee,
    Wherewith whole showls of *Martyrs* once did burn,
    Besides their other flames? Doth Poetry
Wear *Venus* Livery? only serve her turn?
Why are not *Sonnets* made of thee? and layes
    Upon thine Altar burnt? Cannot thy love
    Heighten a spirit to sound out thy praise
As well as any she? Cannot thy *Dove*
Out strip their *Cupid* easily in flight?
    Or, since thy wayes are deep, and still the same,
    Will not a verse run smooth that bears thy name?
Why doth that fire, which by thy power and might
    Each breast does feel, no braver fuel choose
    Than that, which one day Worms may chance refuse?

Sure, Lord, there is enough in thee to dry
    Oceans of *Ink*; for, as the Deluge did
    Cover the Earth, so doth thy Majesty:
Each Cloud distills thy praise, and doth forbid
Poets to turn it to another use.
    Roses and *Lillies* speak thee; and to make
    A pair of Cheeks of them, is thy abuse.
Why should I *Womens eyes* for Chrystal take?
Such poor invention burns in their low mind
    Whose fire is wild, and doth not upward go
    To praise, and on thee, Lord, some *Ink* bestow.
Open the bones, and you shall nothing find
    In the best *face* but *filth*, when, Lord, in thee
    The *beauty* lies in the *discovery*.

Redemption

Having been tenant long to a rich Lord,
   Not thriving, I resolved to be bold,
   And make a suit unto him, to afford
A new small-rented lease, and cancel th' old.

In Heaven at his manor I him sought:
   They told me there, that he was lately gone
   About some land, which he had dearly bought
Long since on earth, to take possession.

I straight return'd, and knowing his great birth,
   Sought him accordingly in great resorts;
   In cities, theatres, gardens, parks, and courts:
At length I heard a ragged noise and mirth

     Of thieves and murderers: there I him espied,
     Who straight, *Your suit is granted*, said, and died.

Prayer

Prayer, the Church's banquet, Angel's age,
   God's breath in man returning to his birth,
   The soul in paraphrase, heart in pilgrimage,
The Christian plummet sounding heaven and earth;

Engine against th'Almighty, sinner's tower,
   Reversed thunder, Christ-side-piercing spear,
   The six days' world-transposing in an hour,
A kind of tune, which all things hear and fear;

Softness, and peace, and joy, and love, and bliss,
   Exalted Manna, gladness of the best,
   Heaven in ordinary, men well drest,
The Milky Way, the bird of Paradise,

     Church-bells beyond the stars heard, the soul's blood,
     The land of spices, something understood.

Love (I)

Immortall Love, authour of this great frame,
　　Sprung from that beautie which can never fade;
　　How hath man parcel'd out thy glorious name,
And thrown it on that dust which thou hast made,
While mortall love doth all the title gain!
　　Which siding with invention, they together
　　Bear all the sway, possessing heart and brain,
(Thy workmanship) and give thee share in neither.
Wit fancies beautie, beautie raiseth wit:
　　The world is theirs; they two play out the game,
　　Thou standing by: and though thy glorious name
Wrought our deliverance from th' infernall pit,
　　Who sings thy praise? onely a skarf or glove
　　Doth warm our hands, and make them write of love.

The H. Scriptures (I)

Oh Book! infinite sweetnesse! let my heart
　　Suck ev'ry letter, and a hony gain,
　　Precious for any grief in any part;
To cleare the breast, to mollifie all pain.
Thou art all health, healty thriving till it make
　　A full eternitie: thou art a masse
　　Of strange delights, where we may wish & take.
Ladies, look here; this is the thankfull glasse,
That mends the lookers eyes: this is the well
　　That washes what it shows. Who can indeare
　　Thy praise too much? thou art heav'ns Lidger here,
Working against the states of death and hell.
　　Thou art joyes handsell: heav'n lies flat in thee,
　　Subject to ev'ry mounters bended knee.

The H. Scriptures (II)

Oh that I knew how all thy lights combine,
    And the configurations of their glorie!
    Seeing not onely how each verse doth shine,
But all the constellations of the storie.
This verse marks that, and both do make a motion
    Unto a third, that ten leaves off doth lie:
    Then as dispersed herbs do watch a potion,
These three make up some Christians destinie:
Such are thy secrets, which my life makes good,
    And comments on thee: for in ev'ry thing
    Thy words do finde me out, & parallels bring,
And in another make me understood.
    Starres are poore books, & oftentimes do misse:
    This book of starres lights to eternall blisse.

JOHN MILTON

O Nightingale!

O Nightingale! that on yon bloomy spray
    Warblest at eve, when all the woods are still,
    Thou with fresh hope the lover's heart dost fill,
    While the jolly hours lead on propitious May.
Thy liquid notes that close the eye of day,
    First heard before the shallow cuckoo's bill,
    Portend success in love. O, if Jove's will
    Have linked that amorous power to thy soft lay,
Now timely sing, ere the rude bird of hate
    Foretell my hopeless doom, in some grove nigh;
    As thou from year to year hast sung too late
For my relief, yet hadst no reason why.
    Whether the Muse or Love call thee his mate,
    Both them I serve, and of their train am I.

How Soon Hath Time

How soon hath Time, the subtle thief of youth,
    Stoln on his wing my three and twentieth year!
    My hasting days fly on with full career,
    But my late spring no bud or blossom shew'th.
Perhaps my semblance might deceive the truth,
    That I to manhood am arrived so near,
    And inward ripeness doth much less appear,
    That some more timely-happy spirits endu'th.
Yet be it less or more, or soon or slow,
    It shall be still in strictest measure even
    To that same lot, however mean or high,
Toward which Time leads me, and the will of Heaven;
    All is, if I have grace to use it so,
    As ever in my great Taskmaster's eye.

On the New Forcers of Conscience Under the Long Parliament

Because you have thrown off your prelate lord,
    And with stiff vows renounced his liturgy,
    To seize the widowed whore Plurality
    From them whose sin ye envied, not abhorred,
Dare ye for this adjure the civil sword
    To force our consciences that Christ set free,
    And ride us with a classic hierarchy
    Taught ye by mere A. S. and Rutherford?
Men whose life, learning, faith and pure intent
    Would have been held in high esteem with Paul
    Must now be named and printed heretics
By shallow Edwards and Scotch what d'ye call:
    But we do hope to find out all your tricks,
    Your plots and packings worse than those of Trent,
                That so the Parliament
May with their wholesome and preventive shears
Clip your phylacteries, though balk your ears,
                And succor our just fears
When they shall read this clearly in your charge
New *presbyter* is but old *priest* writ large.

To the Lord General Cromwell

Cromwell, our chief of men, who through a cloud,
    Not of war only, but detractions rude,
    Guided by faith and matchless fortitude,
    To peace and truth thy glorious way hast ploughed,
And on the neck of crownèd Fortune proud
    Hast reared God's trophies, and His work pursued,
    While Darwen stream, with blood of Scots imbrued,
    And Dunbar field, resounds thy praises loud,
And Worcester's laureate wreath: yet much remains
    To conquer still; peace hath her victories
    No less renowned than war: new foes arise,
Threatening to bind our souls with secular chains.
    Help us to save free conscience from the paw
    Of hireling wolves, whose gospel is their maw.

On the Late Massacre in Piedmont

Avenge, O Lord, thy slaughtered Saints, whose bones
    Lie scattered on the Alpine mountains cold,
    Even them who kept thy truth so pure of old
    When all our Fathers worshiped Stocks and Stones,
Forget not: in thy book record their groans
    Who were thy Sheep and in their ancient Fold
    Slain by the bloody *Piedmontese* that rolled
    Mother with infant down the Rocks. Their moans
The Vales redoubled to the Hills, and they
    To Heaven. Their martyred blood and ashes sow
    O'er all th' *Italian* fields where still doth sway
The triple Tyrant: that from these may grow
    A hundredfold, who having learnt thy way
    Early may fly the *Babylonian* woe.

"When I consider how my light is spent"

When I consider how my light is spent,
    Ere half my days, in this dark world and wide,
    And that one Talent which is death to hide
    Lodg'd with me useless, though my Soul more bent
To serve therewith my Maker, and present
    My true account, lest he returning chide,
    Doth God exact day-labour, light deny'd,
    I fondly ask; but patience to prevent
That murmur, soon replies, God does not need
    Either man's work or his own gifts, who best
    Bear his milde yoak, they serve him best, his State
Is Kingly. Thousands at his bidding speed
    And post o're Land and Ocean without rest:
    They also serve who only stand and waite.

"Methought I saw my late espousèd Saint"

Methought I saw my late espousèd Saint
    Brought to me like Alcestis from the grave,
    Whom Jove's great son to her glad husband gave,
    Rescued from death by force, though pale and faint.
Mine, as whom washt from spot of child-bed taint
    Purification in the Old Law did save,
    And such, as yet once more I trust to have
    Full sight of her in Heaven without restraint,
Came vested all in white, pure as her mind.
    Her face was veiled; yet to my fancied sight
    Love, sweetness, goodness, in her person shined
So clear as in no face with more delight.
    But O, as to embrace me she inclined,
    I waked, she fled, and day brought back my night.

CHARLES COTTON

from *Resolution in Four Sonnets, of a Poetical Question Put to Me by a Friend, Concerning Four Rural Sisters*

1

Alice is tall and upright as a pine,
White as blanched almonds, or the falling snow,
Sweet as are damask roses when they blow,
And doubtless fruitful as the swelling vine.

Ripe to be cut, and ready to be pressed,
Her full cheeked beauties very well appear,
And a year's fruit she loses every year,
Wanting a man t' improve her to the best.

Full fain she would be husbanded, and yet,
Alas! she cannot a fit laborer get
To cultivate her to her own content:

Fain would she be (God wot) about her task,
And yet (forsooth) she is too proud to ask,
And (which is worse) too modest to consent.

2

Marg'ret of humbler stature by the head
Is (as it oft falls out with yellow hair)
Than her fair sister, yet so much more fair,
As her pure white is better mixed with red.

This, hotter than the other ten to one,
Longs to be put unto her mother's trade,
And loud proclaims she lives too long a maid,
Wishing for one t' untie her virgin zone.

She finds virginity a kind of ware,
That's very very troublesome to bear,
And being gone, she thinks will ne'er be mist:

And yet withal, the girl has so much grace,
To call for help I know she wants the face,
Though asked, I know not how she would resist.

3
Mary is black, and taller than the last,
Yet equal in perfection and desire,
To the one's melting snow, and t' other's fire,
As with whose black their fairness is defaced.

She pants as much for love as th' other two,
But she so virtuous is, or else so wise,
That she will win or will not love a prize,
And upon but good terms will never do:

Therefore, who her will conquer ought to be
At least as full of love and wit as she,
Or he shall ne'er gain favor at her hands:

Nay, though he have a pretty store of brains,
Shall only have his labor for his pains,
Unless he offer more than she demands.

THOMAS GRAY

On the Death of Mr. Richard West

In vain to me the smiling mornings shine,
And redd'ning Phoebus lifts his golden fire:
The birds in vain their amorous descant join;
Or cheerful fields resume their green attire:
These ears, alas! for other notes repine,
A different object do these eyes require.
My lonely anguish melts no heart but mine;
And in my breast the imperfect joys expire.
Yet morning smiles the busy race to cheer,
And new-born pleasure brings to happier men:
The fields to all their wonted tribute bear:
To warm their little loves the birds complain:
I fruitless mourn to him, that cannot hear,
And weep the more, because I weep in vain.

CHARLOTTE SMITH

To the Moon

Queen of the silver bow!—by thy pale beam,
Alone and pensive, I delight to stray,
And watch thy shadow trembling in the stream,
Or mark the floating clouds that cross thy way.
And while I gaze, thy mild and placid light
Sheds a soft calm upon my troubled breast;
And oft I think—fair planet of the night—
That in thy orb, the wretched may have rest:
The sufferers of the earth perhaps may go,
Released by Death—to thy benignant sphere,
And the sad children of Despair and Woe
Forget, in thee, their cup of sorrow here.
Oh! that I soon may reach thy world serene,
Poor wearied pilgrim—in this toiling scene!

Written Near a Port on a Dark Evening

Huge vapors brood above the clifted shore,
    Night on the ocean settles, dark and mute,
Save where is heard the repercussive roar
    Of drowsy billows, on the rugged foot
Of rocks remote; or still more distant tone
    Of seamen in the anchored bark that tell
The watch relieved; or one deep voice alone
    Singing the hour, and bidding "Strike the bell."
All is black shadow, but the lucid line
    Marked by the light surf on the level sand,
Or where afar the ship-lights faintly shine
    Like wandering fairy fires, that oft on land
Mislead the pilgrim—such the dubious ray
That wavering reason lends, in life's long darkling way.

WILLIAM BLAKE

To the Evening Star

Thou fair-hair'd angel of the evening,
Now, while the sun rests on the mountains, light
Thy bright torch of love; thy radiant crown
Put on, and smile upon our evening bed!
Smile on our loves; and, while thou drawest the
Blue curtains of the sky, scatter thy silver dew
On every flower that shuts its sweet eyes
In timely sleep. Let thy west wind sleep on
The lake; speak silence with thy glimmering eyes,
And wash the dusk with silver. Soon, full soon,
Dost thou withdraw; then the wolf rages wide,
And the lion glares thro' the dun forest:
The fleeces of our flocks are cover'd with
Thy sacred dew: protect them with thine influence.

ROBERT BURNS

A Sonnet upon Sonnets

Fourteen, a sonneteer thy praises sings;
What magic myst'ries in that number lie!
Your hen hath fourteen eggs beneath her wings
That fourteen chickens to the roost may fly.
Fourteen full pounds the jockey's stone must be;
His age fourteen—a horse's prime is past.
Fourteen long hours too oft the Bard must fast;
Fourteen bright bumpers—bliss he ne'er must see!
Before fourteen, a dozen yields the strife;
Before fourteen—e'en thirteen's strength is vain.
Fourteen good years—a woman gives us life;
Fourteen good men—we lose that life again.
What lucubrations can be more upon it?
Fourteen good measur'd verses make a sonnet.

WILLIAM WORDSWORTH

"Nuns fret not at their convent's narrow room"

Nuns fret not at their convent's narrow room;
And hermits are contented with their cells;
And students with their pensive citadels;
Maids at the wheel, the weaver at his loom,
Sit blithe and happy; bees that soar for bloom,
High as the highest Peak of Furness-fells,
Will murmur by the hour in foxglove bells:
In truth the prison, unto which we doom
Ourselves, no prison is: and hence for me,
In sundry moods, 'twas pastime to be bound
Within the Sonnet's scanty plot of ground;
Pleased if some Souls (for such there needs must be)
Who have felt the weight of too much liberty,
Should find brief solace there, as I have found.

Composed upon Westminster Bridge, September 3, 1802

Earth has not anything to show more fair:
Dull would he be of soul who could pass by
A sight so touching in its majesty:
This City now doth, like a garment, wear
The beauty of the morning; silent, bare,
Ships, towers, domes, theatres, and temples lie
Open unto the fields, and to the sky;
All bright and glittering in the smokeless air.
Never did sun more beautifully steep
In his first splendour, valley, rock, or hill;
Ne'er saw I, never felt, a calm so deep!
The river glideth at his own sweet will:
Dear God! the very houses seem asleep;
And all that mighty heart is lying still!

The world is too much with us; late and soon

The world is too much with us; late and soon,
Getting and spending, we lay waste our powers:
Little we see in Nature that is ours;
We have given our hearts away, a sordid boon!
This sea that bares her bosom to the moon;
The winds that will be howling at all hours
And are up-gathered now like sleeping flowers;
For this, for every thing, we are out of tune;
It moves us not—Great God! I'd rather be
A Pagan suckled in a creed outworn;
So might I, standing on this pleasant lea,
Have glimpses that would make me less forlorn;
Have sight of Proteus coming from the sea;
Or hear old Triton blow his wreathed horn.

It is a beauteous evening, calm and free

It is a beauteous evening, calm and free;
The holy time is quiet as a nun
Breathless with adoration; the broad sun
Is sinking down in its tranquillity;
The gentleness of heaven is on the Sea:
Listen! the mighty Being is awake,
And doth with his eternal motion make
A sound like thunder—everlastingly.
Dear Child! dear Girl! that walkest with me here,
If thou appear'st untouched by solemn thought,
Thy nature is not therefore less divine:
Thou liest in Abraham's bosom all the year;
And worshipp'st at the Temple's inner shrine,
God being with thee when we know it not.

from *Sonnets Dedicated to Liberty*

To Toussaint L'Ouverture

Toussaint, the most unhappy Man of Men!
Whether the rural milk-maid by her cow
Sing in thy hearing, or thou liest now
Alone in some deep dungeon's earless den,
O miserable chieftain! where and when
Wilt thou find patience? Yet die not; do thou
Wear rather in thy bonds a cheerful brow:
Though fallen thyself, never to rise again,
Live, and take comfort. Thou hast left behind
Powers that will work for thee; air, earth, and skies;
There's not a breathing of the common wind
That will forget thee; thou hast great allies;
Thy friends are exultations, agonies,
And love, and Man's unconquerable mind.

London, 1802

Milton! thou should'st be living at this hour:
England hath need of thee: she is a fen
Of stagnant waters: altar, sword and pen,
Fireside, the heroic wealth of hall and bower,
Have forfeited their ancient English dower
Of inward happiness. We are selfish men;
Oh! raise us up, return to us again;
And give us manners, virtue, freedom, power.
Thy soul was like a star and dwelt apart:
Thou hadst a voice whose sound was like the sea;
Pure as the naked heavens, majestic, free,
So didst thou travel on life's common way,
In cheerful godliness; and yet thy heart
The lowliest duties on itself did lay.

"Surprised by joy—impatient as the wind"

Surprised by joy—impatient as the wind
I turned to share the transport—Oh! with whom
But thee, long buried in the silent tomb,
That spot which no vicissitude can find?
Love, faithful love, recalled thee to my mind—
But how could I forget thee?—Through what power,
Even for the least division of an hour,
Have I been so beguiled as to be blind
To my most grievous loss?—That thought's return
Was the worst pang that sorrow ever bore,
Save one, one only, when I stood forlorn,
Knowing my heart's best treasure was no more;
That neither present time, nor years unborn
Could to my sight that heavenly face restore.

"Scorn not the Sonnet; critic, you have frowned"

Scorn not the Sonnet; critic, you have frowned,
Mindless of its just honors;—with this key
Shakespeare unlocked his heart; the melody
Of this small lute gave ease to Petrarch's wound;
A thousand times this pipe did Tasso sound;
Camöens soothed with it an exile's grief;
The Sonnet glittered a gay myrtle leaf
Amid the cypress with which Dante crowned
His visionary brow: a glow-worm lamp,
It cheered mild Spenser, called from Faery-land
To struggle through dark ways; and when a damp
Fell round the path of Milton, in his hand
The thing became a trumpet, whence he blew
Soul-animating strains—alas, too few!

SAMUEL TAYLOR COLERIDGE

To the River Otter

Dear native brook! wild streamlet of the West!
How many various-fated years have passed,
What happy, and what mournful hours, since last
I skimmed the smooth thin stone along thy breast,
Numbering its light leaps! Yet so deep imprest
Sink the sweet scenes of childhood, that mine eyes
I never shut amid the sunny ray,
But straight with all their tints thy waters rise,
Thy crossing plank, thy marge with willows gray,
And bedded sand that, veined with various dyes,
Gleamed through thy bright transparence. On my way,
Visions of childhood! oft have ye beguiled
Lone manhood's cares, yet waking fondest sighs:
Ah! that once more I were a careless child.

To Nature

It may indeed be phantasy when I
Essay to draw from all created things
Deep, heartfelt, inward joy that closely clings;
And trace in leaves and flowers that round me lie
Lessons of love and earnest piety.
So let it be; and if the wide world rings
In mock of this belief, to me it brings
Nor fear, nor grief, nor vain perplexity.
So will I build my altar in the fields,
And the blue sky my fretted dome shall be,
And the sweet fragrance that the wild flower yields
Shall be the incense I will yield to Thee,
Thee only God! and Thou shalt not despise
Even me, the priest of this poor sacrifice.

Work Without Hope

All Nature seems at work. Slugs leave their lair—
The bees are stirring—birds are on the wing—
And Winter, slumbering in the open air,
Wears on his smiling face a dream of Spring!
And I, the while, the sole unbusy thing,
Nor honey make, nor pair, nor build, nor sing.

Yet well I ken the banks where amaranths blow,
Have traced the fount where streams of nectar flow.
Bloom, O ye amaranths! bloom for whom ye may,
For me ye bloom not! Glide, rich streams, away!
With lips unbrighten'd, wreathless brow, I stroll:
And would you learn the spells that drowse my soul?
Work without Hope draws nectar in a sieve,
And Hope without an object cannot live.

ROBERT SOUTHEY

from *Poems on the Slave Trade*

VI

High in the air exposed the slave is hung
    To all the birds of Heaven, their living food!
He groans not, though awaked by that fierce sun
    New torturers live to drink their parent blood!
He groans not, though the gorging vulture tear
    The quivering fiber! Hither gaze O ye
    Who tore this man from peace and liberty!
Gaze hither ye who weigh with scrupulous care
The right and prudent; for beyond the grave
    There is another world! and call to mind,
    Ere your decrees proclaim to all mankind
Murder is legalized, that there the slave
Before the Eternal, "thunder-tongued shall plead
Against the deep damnation of your deed."

MARY F. JOHNSON

The Idiot Girl

Start not at her, who, in fantastic guise,
    Comes wildly chanting in a dirge-like tone,
With big tears trembling in her vacant eyes,
    And uncoifed tresses by the breezes blown.
Recoil not from the harmless idiot maid,
    Who often from a rugged beldame creeps
To yon deserted cottage in the shade,
    And its fallen stones, to guard the entrance, heaps.
There was the home where passed her early years
    With parents now withdrawn to final rest,
Who proved how infant helplessness endears;
    And of a numerous offspring loved her best.
Now wails she, as she rudely blocks the door,
"They both are in, and will come out no more."

LEIGH HUNT

To the Grasshopper and the Cricket

Green little vaulter in the sunny grass,
    Catching your heart up at the feel of June,
    Sole voice that's heard amidst the lazy noon,
When even the bees lag at the summoning brass;
And you, warm little housekeeper, who class
    With those who think the candles come too soon,
    Loving the fire, and with your tricksome tune
Nick the glad silent moments as they pass;
O, sweet and tiny cousin! that belong,
    One to the fields, the other to the hearth,
Both have your sunshine; both though small are strong
    At your clear hearts; and both were sent on earth
To sing in thoughtful ears this natural song:
    In doors and out, summer and winter, Mirth.

GEORGE GORDON, LORD BYRON

On Chillon

Eternal spirit of the chainless mind!
   Brightest in dungeons, Liberty! thou art,
   For there thy habitation is the heart—
The heart which love of thee alone can bind;
And when thy sons to fetters are consigned—
   To fetters, and the damp vault's dayless gloom,
   Their country conquers with their martyrdom,
And Freedom's fame finds wings on every wind.
Chillon! thy prison is a holy place,
   And thy sad floor an altar—for 'twas trod,
Until his very steps have left a trace
   Worn, as if thy cold pavement were a sod,
By Bonnivard!—May none those marks efface!
   For they appeal from tyranny to God.

"Rousseau—Voltaire—our Gibbon—and de Staël"

Rousseau—Voltaire—our Gibbon—and de Staël—
   Leman! these names are worthy of thy shore,
   Thy shore of names like these! wert thou no more,
Their memory thy remembrance would recall:
To them thy banks were lovely as to all,
   But they have made them lovelier, for the lore
   Of mighty minds doth hallow in the core
Of human hearts the ruin of a wall
   Where dwelt the wise and wondrous; but by *thee*
How much more, Lake of Beauty! do we feel,
   In sweetly gliding o'er thy crystal sea,
The wild glow of that not ungentle zeal,
   Which of the heirs of immortality
Is proud, and makes the breath of glory real!

PERCY BYSSHE SHELLEY

Ozymandias

I met a traveller from an antique land
Who said: Two vast and trunkless legs of stone
Stand in the desert. Near them, on the sand,
Half sunk, a shattered visage lies, whose frown,
And wrinkled lip, and sneer of cold command,
Tell that its sculptor well those passions read
Which yet survive, stamped on these lifeless things,
The hand that mocked them and the heart that fed;
And on the pedestal these words appear:
"My name is Ozymandias, king of kings:
Look on my works, ye Mighty, and despair!"
Nothing beside remains. Round the decay
Of that colossal wreck, boundless and bare
The lone and level sands stretch far away.

England in 1819

An old, mad, blind, despised, and dying king,—
Princes, the dregs of their dull race, who flow
Through public scorn,—mud from a muddy spring,—
Rulers who neither see, nor feel, nor know,
But leech-like to their fainting country cling,
Till they drop, blind in blood, without a blow,—
A people starved and stabbed in the untilled field,—
An army, which liberticide and prey
Makes as a two-edged sword to all who wield,—
Golden and sanguine laws which tempt and slay;
Religion Christless, Godless—a book sealed;
A Senate,—Time's worst statute unrepealed,—
Are graves, from which a glorious Phantom may
Burst, to illumine our tempestuous day.

JOHN CLARE

To Wordsworth

Wordsworth I love, his books are like the fields,
    Not filled with flowers, but works of human kind;
The pleasant weed a fragrant pleasure yields,
    The briar and broomwood shaken by the wind,
The thorn and bramble o'er the water shoot
    A finer flower than gardens e'er gave birth,
The aged huntsman grubbing up the root—
    I love them all as tenants of the earth:
Where genius is, there often die the seeds;
    What critics throw away I love the more;
I love to stoop and look among the weeds,
    To find a flower I never knew before;
Wordsworth, go on—a greater poet be;
Merit will live, though parties disagree!

Hen's Nest

Among the orchard weeds, from every search,
Snugly and sure, the old hen's nest is made,
Who cackles every morning from her perch
To tell the servant girl new eggs are laid;
Who lays her washing by; and far and near
Goes seeking all about from day to day,
And stung with nettles tramples everywhere;
But still the cackling pullet lays away.
The boy on Sundays goes the stack to pull
In hopes to find her there, but naught is seen,
And takes his hat and thinks to find it full,
She's laid so long so many might have been.
But naught is found and all is given o'er
Till the young brood come chirping to the door.

The Happy Bird

The happy white-throat on the swaying bough,
Rocked by the impulse of the gadding wind
That ushers in the showers of April, now
Carols right joyously; and now reclined,
Crouching, she clings close to her moving seat,
To keep her hold;—and till the wind for rest
Pauses, she mutters inward melodies,
That seem her heart's rich thinkings to repeat.
But when the branch is still, her little breast
Swells out in rapture's gushing symphonies;
And then, against her brown wing softly prest,
The wind comes playing, an enraptured guest;
This way and that she swings—till gusts arise
More boisterous in their play, then off she flies.

The Thrush's Nest

Within a thick and spreading hawthorn bush,
That overhung a molehill large and round,
I heard from morn to morn a merry thrush
Sing hymns to sunrise, and I drank the sound
With joy, and, often an intruding guest,
I watched her secret toils from day to day—
How true she warped the moss, to form a nest,
And modelled it within with wood and clay;
And by and by, like heath-bells gilt with dew,
There lay her shining eggs, as bright as flowers,
Ink-spotted-over shells of greeny blue:
And there I witnessed in the sunny hours
A brood of nature's minstrels chirp and fly,
Glad as that sunshine and the laughing sky.

JOHN KEATS

On First Looking into Chapman's Homer

Much have I travell'd in the realms of gold,
    And many goodly states and kingdoms seen;
    Round many western islands have I been
Which bards in fealty to Apollo hold.
Oft of one wide expanse had I been told
    That deep-brow'd Homer ruled as his demesne;
    Yet did I never breathe its pure serene
Till I heard Chapman speak out loud and bold:
Then felt I like some watcher of the skies
    When a new planet swims into his ken;
Or like stout Cortez when with eagle eyes
    He star'd at the Pacific—and all his men
Look'd at each other with a wild surmise—
    Silent, upon a peak in Darien.

On the Grasshopper and Cricket

The poetry of earth is never dead:
    When all the birds are faint with the hot sun,
    And hide in cooling trees, a voice will run
From hedge to hedge about the new-mown mead;
That is the Grasshopper's—he takes the lead
    In summer luxury,—he has never done
    With his delights; for when tired out with fun
He rests at ease beneath some pleasant weed.
The poetry of earth is ceasing never:
    On a lone winter evening, when the frost
    Has wrought a silence, from the stove there shrills
The Cricket's song, in warmth increasing ever,
    And seems to one in drowsiness half lost,
    The Grasshopper's among some grassy hills.

"When I have fears that I may cease to be"

When I have fears that I may cease to be
   Before my pen has glean'd my teeming brain,
Before high piled books, in charactry,
   Hold like rich garners the full ripen'd grain;
When I behold, upon the night's starr'd face,
   Huge cloudy symbols of a high romance,
And think that I may never live to trace
   Their shadows, with the magic hand of chance;
And when I feel, fair creature of an hour,
   That I shall never look upon thee more,
Never have relish in the fairy power
   Of unreflecting love;—then on the shore
Of the wide world I stand alone, and think
Till love and fame to nothingness do sink.

"Bright star, would I were stedfast as thou art"

Bright star, would I were stedfast as thou art—
   Not in lone splendor hung aloft the night,
And watching, with eternal lids apart,
   Like nature's patient, sleepless eremite,
The moving waters at their priestlike task
   Of pure ablution round earth's human shores,
Or gazing on the new soft-fallen mask
   Of snow upon the mountains and the moors;
No—yet still stedfast, still unchangeable,
   Pillow'd upon my fair love's ripening breast,
To feel for ever its soft swell and fall,
   Awake for ever in a sweet unrest,
Still, still to hear her tender-taken breath,
And so live ever—or else swoon to death.

Sonnet to Sleep

O soft embalmer of the still midnight,
    Shutting with careful fingers and benign
Our gloom-pleas'd eyes, embower'd from the light,
    Enshaded in forgetfulness divine:
O soothest Sleep! if so it please thee, close,
    In midst of this thine hymn, my willing eyes,
Or wait the Amen ere thy poppy throws
    Around my bed its lulling charities.
Then save me or the passed day will shine
    Upon my pillow, breeding many woes:
Save me from curious conscience, that still hoards
    Its strength for darkness, burrowing like the mole;
Turn the key deftly in the oiled wards,
    And seal the hushed casket of my soul.

"If by dull rhymes our English must be chain'd"

If by dull rhymes our English must be chain'd,
    And, like Andromeda, the sonnet sweet
        Fetter'd, in spite of pained loveliness;
Let us find out, if we must be constrain'd,
    Sandals more interwoven and complete
To fit the naked foot of Poesy;
        Let us inspect the lyre, and weigh the stress
Of every chord, and see what may be gain'd
    By ear industrious, and attention meet;
        Misers of sound and syllable, no less
Than Midas of his coinage, let us be
    Jealous of dead leaves in the bay wreath crown;
So, if we may not let the muse be free,
    She will be bound with garlands of her own.

HARTLEY COLERIDGE

"Let me not deem that I was made in vain"

Let me not deem that I was made in vain,
Or that my being was an accident
Which Fate, in working its sublime intent,
Not wished to be, to hinder would not deign.
Each drop uncounted in a storm of rain
Hath its own mission, and is duly sent
To its own leaf or blade, not idly spent
'Mid myriad dimples on the shipless main.
The very shadow of an insect's wing,
For which the violet cared not while it stayed,
Yet felt the lighter for its vanishing,
Proved that the sun was shining by its shade.
Then can a drop of the eternal spring,
Shadow of living lights, in vain be made?

"Think upon Death, 'tis good to think of Death"

Think upon Death, 'tis good to think of Death,
But better far to think upon the Dead.
Death is a spectre with a bony head,
Or the mere mortal body without breath,
The state foredoomed of every son of Seth,
Decomposition—dust, or dreamless sleep.
But the dear Dead are they for whom we weep,
For whom I credit all the Bible saith.
Dead is my father, dead is my good mother,
And what on earth have I to do but die?
But if by grace I reach the blessed sky,
I fain would see the same, and not another;
The very father that I used to see,
The mother that has nursed me on her knee.

THOMAS LOVELL BEDDOES

To Night

So thou art come again, old black-winged night,
    Like a huge bird, between us and the sun,
Hiding, with out-stretched form, the genial light;
    And still, beneath thine icy bosom's dun
And cloudy plumage, hatching fog-breathed blight,
    And embryo storms, and crabbed frosts, that shun
Day's warm caress. The owls from ivied loop
    Are shrieking homage, as thou cowerest high,
Like sable crow pausing in eager stoop
    On the dim world thou gluttest thy clouded eye,
Silently waiting latest time's fell whoop,
    When thou shalt quit thine eyrie in the sky,
To pounce upon the world with eager claw,
And tomb time, death, and substance in thy maw.

ELIZABETH BARRETT BROWNING

Finite and Infinite

The wind sounds only in opposing straits,
The sea, beside the shore; man's spirit rends
Its quiet only up against the ends
Of wants and oppositions, loves and hates,
Where, worked and worn by passionate debates,
And losing by the loss it apprehends,
The flesh rocks round, and every breath it sends
Is ravelled to a sigh. All tortured states
Suppose a straitened place. Jehovah Lord,
Make room for rest, around me! out of sight
Now float me, of the vexing land abhorred,
Till in deep calms of space my soul may right
Her nature,—shoot large sail on lengthening cord,
And rush exultant on the Infinite.

from *Sonnets from the Portuguese*

VII

The face of all the world is changed, I think,
Since first I heard the footsteps of thy soul
Move still, oh, still, beside me; as they stole
Betwixt me and the dreadful outer brink
Of obvious death, where I who thought to sink
Was caught up into love, and taught the whole
Of life in a new rhythm. The cup of dole
God gave for baptism, I am fain to drink,
And praise its sweetness, sweet, with thee anear.
The names of country, heaven, are changed away
For where thou art or shalt be, there or here;
And this—this lute and song—loved yesterday,
(The singing angels know) are only dear,
Because thy name moves right in what they say.

XIII

And wilt thou have me fashion into speech
The love I bear thee, finding words enough,
And hold the torch out, while the winds are rough,
Between our faces, to cast light on each?—
I drop it at thy feet. I cannot teach
My hand to hold my spirit so far off
From myself—me—that I should bring thee proof
In words, of love hid in me out of reach.
Nay, let the silence of my womanhood
Commend my woman-love to thy belief,—
Seeing that I stand unwon, however wooed,
And rend the garment of my life, in brief,
By a most dauntless, voiceless fortitude,
Lest one touch of this heart convey its grief.

XVIII

I never gave a lock of hair away
To a man, Dearest, except this to thee,
Which now upon my fingers thoughtfully,
I ring out to the full brown length and say
"Take it." My day of youth went yesterday;
My hair no longer bounds to my foot's glee,
Nor plant I it from rose or myrtle-tree,
As girls do, any more. It only may
Now shade on two pale cheeks, the mark of tears,
Taught drooping from the head that hangs aside
Through sorrow's trick. I thought the funeral-shears
Would take this first; but Love is justified:
Take it thou,—finding pure, from all those years,
The kiss my mother left here when she died.

XLII

How do I love thee? Let me count the ways.
I love thee to the depth and breadth and height
My soul can reach, when feeling out of sight
For the ends of Being and Ideal Grace.
I love thee to the level of everyday's
Most quiet need, by sun and candlelight.
I love thee freely, as men strive for Right;
I love thee purely, as they turn from Praise;
I love thee with the passion put to use
In my own griefs, and with my childhood's faith;
I love thee with a love I seemed to lose
With my lost saints,—I love thee with the breath,
Smiles, tears, of all my life!—and, if God choose,
I shall but love thee better after death.

HENRY WADSWORTH LONGFELLOW

Chaucer

An old man in a lodge within a park;
    The chamber walls depicted all around
      With portraitures of huntsman, hawk, and hound,
      And the hurt deer. He listeneth to the lark,
Whose song comes with the sunshine through the dark
    Of painted glass in leaden lattice bound;
      He listeneth and he laugheth at the sound,
      Then writeth in a book like any clerk.
He is the poet of the dawn, who wrote
    The Canterbury Tales, and his old age
      Made beautiful with song; and as I read
I hear the crowing cock, I hear the note
    Of lark and linnet, and from every page
      Rise odors of ploughed field or flowery mead.

CHARLES TENNYSON TURNER

Letty's Globe

When Letty had scarce passed her third glad year,
And her young artless words began to flow,
One day we gave the child a coloured sphere
Of the wide earth, that she might mark and know,
By tint and outline, all its sea and land.
She patted all the world; old empires peeped
Between her baby fingers. Her soft hand
Was welcome at all frontiers. How she leaped,
And laughed, and prattled, in her world-wide bliss.
But when we turned her sweet unlearned eye
On our own isle, she raised a joyous cry,
'Oh! yes, I see it. Letty's home is there!'
And while she hid all England with a kiss,
Bright over Europe fell her golden hair.

EDGAR ALLAN POE

To Science

Science, true daughter of Old Time thou art!
    Who alterest all things with thy peering eyes.
Why preyest thou thus upon the poet's heart,
    Vulture, whose wings are dull realities?
How should he love thee, or how deem thee wise,
    Who wouldst not leave him in his wandering
To seek for treasure in the jeweled skies,
    Albeit he soared with an undaunted wing?
Hast thou not dragged Diana from her car,
    And driven the Hamadryad from the wood
To seek a shelter in some happier star?
    Hast thou not torn the Naiad from her flood,
The Elfin from the green grass, and from me
The summer dream beneath the tamarind tree?

ALFRED, LORD TENNYSON

"If I were loved, as I desire to be"

If I were loved, as I desire to be,
What is there in the great sphere of the earth,
And range of evil between death and birth,
That I should fear,—if I were loved by thee?
All the inner, all the outer world of pain
Clear love would pierce and cleave, if thou wert mine,
As I have heard that, somewhere in the main,
Fresh-water springs come up through bitter brine.
'Twere joy, not fear, clasped hand in hand with thee,
To wait for death—mute—careless of all ills,
Apart upon a mountain, though the surge
Of some new deluge from a thousand hills
Flung leagues of roaring foam into the gorge
Below us, as far on as eye could see.

ROBERT BROWNING

Why I Am a Liberal

"Why?" Because all I haply can and do,
    And that I am now, all I hope to be,—
    Whence comes it save from fortune setting free
Body and soul the purpose to pursue,
God traced for both? If fetters not a few,
    Of prejudice, convention, fall from me,
    These shall I bid men—each in his degree
Also God-guided—bear, and gaily, too?
But little do or can the best of us:
    That little is achieved through Liberty.
Who, then, dares hold, emancipated thus,
    His fellow shall continue bound? Not I,
Who live, love, labor freely, nor discuss
    A brother's right to freedom. That is "Why".

AUBREY THOMAS DE VERE

The Sun God

I saw the Master of the Sun. He stood
    High in his luminous car, himself more bright;
    An Archer of immeasurable might:
On his left shoulder hung his quiver'd load;
Spurn'd by his steeds the eastern mountains glowed;
    Forward his eagle eye and bow of Light
He bent, and while both hands that arch embowed,
    Shaft after shaft pursued the flying night.
No wings profaned that godlike form: around
    His neck high held an ever-moving crowd
Of locks hung glistening: while such perfect sound
    Fell from his bowstring that th' ethereal dome
Thrilled as a dew-drop; and each passing cloud
    Expanded, whitening like the ocean foam.

GEORGE ELIOT

from *Brother and Sister*

I

I cannot choose but think upon the time
When our two lives grew like two buds that kiss
At lightest thrill from the bee's swinging chime,
Because the one so near the other is.

He was the elder and a little man
Of forty inches, bound to show no dread,
And I the girl that puppy-like now ran,
Now lagged behind my brother's larger tread.

I held him wise, and when he talked to me
Of snakes and birds, and which God loved the best,
I thought his knowledge marked the boundary
Where men grew blind, though angels knew the rest.

If he said "Hush!" I tried to hold my breath;
Wherever he said "Come!" I stepped in faith.

XI

School parted us; we never found again
That childish world where our two spirits mingled
Like scents from varying roses that remain
One sweetness, nor can evermore be singled.

Yet the twin habit of that early time
Lingered for long about the heart and tongue:
We had been natives of one happy clime,
And its dear accent to our utterance clung,

Till the dire years whose awful name is Change
Had grasped our souls still yearning in divorce,
And pitiless shaped them in two forms that range
Two elements which sever their life's course.

But were another childhood-world my share,
I would be born a little sister there.

FREDERICK GODDARD TUCKERMAN

from *Sonnets, First Series*

10

An upper chamber in a darkened house,
Where, ere his footsteps reached ripe manhood's brink,
Terror and anguish were his lot to drink;
I cannot rid the thought nor hold it close
But dimly dream upon that man alone:
Now though the autumn clouds most softly pass,
The cricket chides beneath the doorstep stone
And greener than the season grows the grass.
Nor can I drop my lids nor shade my brows,
But there he stands beside the lifted sash;
And with a swooning of the heart, I think
Where the black shingles slope to meet the boughs
And, shattered on the roof like smallest snows,
The tiny petals of the mountain ash.

28

Not the round natural world, not the deep mind,
The reconcilement holds: the blue abyss
Collects it not; our arrows sink amiss
And but in Him may we our import find.
The agony to know, the grief, the bliss
Of toil, is vain and vain: clots of the sod
Gathered in heat and haste and flung behind
To blind ourselves and others, what but this
Still grasping dust and sowing toward the wind?
No more thy meaning seek, thine anguish plead,
But leaving straining thought and stammering word,
Across the barren azure pass to God;
Shooting the void in silence like a bird,
A bird that shuts his wings for better speed.

MATTHEW ARNOLD

Shakespeare

Others abide our question. Thou art free.
We ask and ask. Thou smilest and art still,
Out-topping knowledge. For the loftiest hill
Who to the stars uncrowns his majesty,
Planting his steadfast footsteps in the sea,
Making the heaven of heavens his dwelling-place,
Spears but the cloudy border of his base
To the foiled searching of mortality.
And thou, who didst the stars and sunbeams know,
Self-schooled, self-scanned, self-honoured, self-secure,
Didst tread on earth unguessed at. Better so!
All pains the immortal spirit must endure,
All weakness which impairs, all griefs which bow,
Find their sole speech in that victorious brow.

West London

Crouched on the pavement, close by Belgrave Square,
A tramp I saw, ill, moody, and tongue-tied.
A babe was in her arms, and at her side
A girl; their clothes were rags, their feet were bare.

Some laboring men, whose work lay somewhere there,
Passed opposite; she touched her girl, who hied
Across, and begged, and came back satisfied.
The rich she had let pass with frozen stare.

Thought I: "Above her state this spirit towers;
She will not ask of aliens, but of friends,
Of sharers in a common human fate.

"She turns from that cold succor, which attends
The unknown little from the unknowing great,
And points us to a better time than ours."

GEORGE MEREDITH

from *Modern Love*

XVII

At dinner, she is hostess, I am host.
Went the feast ever cheerfuller? She keeps
The Topic over intellectual deeps
In buoyancy afloat. They see no ghost.
With sparkling surface-eyes we ply the ball:
It is in truth a most contagious game:
HIDING THE SKELETON, shall be its name.
Such play as this the devils might appall!
But here's the greater wonder; in that we,
Enamored of an acting naught can tire,
Each other, like true hypocrites, admire;
Warm-lighted looks, Love's ephemeræ,
Shoot gaily o'er the dishes and the wine.
We waken envy of our happy lot.
Fast, sweet, and golden, shows the marriage-knot.
Dear guests, you now have seen Love's corpse-light shine.

XXX

What are we first? First, animals; and next
Intelligences at a leap; on whom
Pale lies the distant shadow of the tomb,
And all that draweth on the tomb for text.
Into which state comes Love, the crowning sun:
Beneath whose light the shadow loses form.
We are the lords of life, and life is warm.
Intelligence and instinct now are one.
But nature says: "My children most they seem
When they least know me: therefore I decree
That they shall suffer." Swift doth young Love flee,
And we stand wakened, shivering from our dream.
Then if we study Nature we are wise.
Thus do the few who live but with the day:
The scientific animals are they—
Lady, this is my sonnet to your eyes.

XXXIV

Madam would speak with me. So, now it comes:
The Deluge or else Fire! She's well; she thanks
My husbandship. Our chain on silence clanks.
Time leers between, above his twiddling thumbs.
Am I quite well? Most excellent in health!
The journals, too, I diligently peruse.
Vesuvius is expected to give news:
Niagara is no noisier. By stealth
Our eyes dart scrutinizing snakes. She's glad
I'm happy, says her quivering under-lip.
"And are not you?" "How can I be?" "Take ship!
For happiness is somewhere to be had."
"Nowhere for me!" Her voice is barely heard.
I am not melted, and make no pretence.
With commonplace I freeze her, tongue and sense.
Niagara or Vesuvius is deferred.

XLVII

We saw the swallows gathering in the sky,
And in the osier-isle we heard them noise.
We had not to look back on summer joys,
Or forward to a summer of bright dye:
But in the largeness of the evening earth
Our spirits grew as we went side by side.
The hour became her husband and my bride.
Love that had robbed us so, thus blessed our dearth!
The pilgrims of the year waxed very loud
In multitudinous chatterings, as the flood
Full brown came from the West, and like pale blood
Expanded to the upper crimson cloud.
Love that had robbed us of immortal things,
This little moment mercifully gave,
Where I have seen across the twilight wave
The swan sail with her young beneath her wings.

Lucifer in Starlight

On a starred night Prince Lucifer uprose.
Tired of his dark dominion swung the fiend
Above the rolling ball in cloud part screened,
Where sinners hugged their spectre of repose.
Poor prey to his hot fit of pride were those.
And now upon his western wing he leaned,
Now his huge bulk o'er Africa careened,
Now the black planet shadowed Arctic snows.
Soaring through wider zones that pricked his scars
With memory of the old revolt from Awe,
He reached a middle height, and at the stars,
Which are the brain of heaven, he looked, and sank.
Around the ancient track marched, rank on rank,
The army of unalterable law.

DANTE GABRIEL ROSSETTI

from *The House of Life*

Introductory Sonnet

A Sonnet is a moment's monument,—
   Memorial from the Soul's eternity
   To one dead deathless hour. Look that it be,
Whether for lustral rite or dire portent,
Or its own arduous fullness reverent:
   Carve it in ivory or in ebony
   As Day or Night shall rule; and let Time see
Its flowering crest impearled and orient.

A Sonnet is a coin: its face reveals
   The soul,—its converse, to what Power 'tis due:—
Whether for tribute to the august appeals
   Of Life, or dower in Love's high retinue
It serve, or, mid the dark wharf's cavernous breath,
In Charon's palm it pay the toll to Death.

XIX. Silent Noon

Your hands lie open in the long fresh grass,—
    The finger-points look through like rosy blooms:
    Your eyes smile peace. The pasture gleams and glooms
'Neath billowing skies that scatter and amass.
All around our nest, far as the eye can pass,
    Are golden kingcup-fields with silver edge
    Where the cow-parsley skirts the hawthorn-hedge.
'Tis visible silence, still as the hour-glass.

Deep in the sun-searched growths the dragon-fly
Hangs like a blue thread loosened from the sky:—
    So this wing'd hour is dropt to us from above.
Oh! clasp we to our hearts, for deathless dower,
This close-companioned inarticulate hour
    When twofold silence was the song of love.

LIII. Without Her

What of her glass without her? the blank grey
    There where the pool is blind of the moon's face.
    Her dress without her? the tossed empty space
Of cloud-rack whence the moon has passed away.
Her paths without her? Day's appointed sway
    Usurped by desolate night. Her pillowed place
    Without her! Tears, Ah me! for love's good grace
And cold forgetfulness, of night or day.

What of the heart without her? Nay, poor heart,
    Of thee what word remains ere speech be still?
    A wayfarer by barren ways and chill,
Steep ways and weary, without her thou art,
Where the long cloud, the long wood's counterpart,
    Sheds doubled darkness up the labouring hill.

LXXXIII. Barren Spring

Once more the changed year's turning wheel returns:
    And as a girl sails balanced in the wind,
    And now before and now again behind
Stoops as it swoops, with cheek that laughs and burns,
So Spring comes merry towards me here, but earns
    No answering smile from me, whose life is twin'd
    With the dead boughs that winter still must bind,
And whom today the Spring no more concerns.

Behold, this crocus is a withering flame;
    This snowdrop, snow; this apple-blossom's part
    To breed the fruit that breeds the serpent's art.
Nay, for these Spring-flowers, turn thy face from them
Nor stay till on the year's last lily-stem
    The white cup shrivels round the golden heart.

XCVII. A Superscription

Look in my face; my name is Might-have-been;
    I am also called No-more, Too-late, Farewell;
Unto thine ear I hold the dead-sea shell
Cast up thy Life's foam-fretted feet between,
Unto thine eyes the glass where that is seen
    Which had Life's form and Love's, but by my spell
    Is now a shaken shadow intolerable,
Of ultimate things unuttered the frail screen.

Mark me, how still I am! But should there dart
    One moment through thy soul the soft surprise
    Of that winged Peace which lulls the breath of sighs,—
Then shalt thou see me smile, and turn apart
Thy visage of mine ambush at thy heart,
    Sleepless, with cold commemorative eyes.

CHRISTINA ROSSETTI

Rest

O Earth, lie heavily upon her eyes;
    Seal her sweet eyes weary of watching, Earth;
    Lie close around her; leave no room for mirth
With its harsh laughter, nor for sound of sighs.
She hath no questions, she hath no replies,
    Hushed in and curtained with a blessèd dearth
    Of all that irked her from the hour of birth;
With stillness that is almost Paradise.
Darkness more clear than noon-day holdeth her,
    Silence more musical than any song;
Even her very heart has ceased to stir:
Until the morning of Eternity
Her rest shall not begin nor end, but be;
    And when she wakes she will not think it long.

In an Artist's Studio

One face looks out from all his canvases,
    One selfsame figure sits or walks or leans:
    We found her hidden just behind those screens,
That mirror gave back all her loveliness.
A queen in opal or in ruby dress,
    A nameless girl in freshest summer-greens,
    A saint, an angel—every canvas means
The same one meaning, neither more nor less.
He feeds upon her face by day and night,
    And she with true kind eyes looks back on him,
Fair as the moon and joyful as the light:
    Not wan with waiting, not with sorrow dim;
Not as she is, but was when hope shone bright;
    Not as she is, but as she fills his dream.

ALGERNON CHARLES SWINBURNE

Cor Cordium

O heart of hearts, the chalice of love's fire,
Hid round with flowers and all the bounty of bloom;
O wonderful and perfect heart, for whom
The lyrist liberty made life a lyre;
O heavenly heart, at whose most dear desire
Dead love, living and singing, cleft his tomb,
And with him risen and regent in death's room
All day thy choral pulses rang full choir;
O heart whose beating blood was running song,
O sole thing sweeter than thine own songs were,
Help us for thy free love's sake to be free,
True for thy truth's sake, for thy strength's sake strong,
Till very liberty make clean and fair
The nursing earth as the sepulchral sea.

THOMAS HARDY

Hap

If but some vengeful god would call to me
From up the sky, and laugh: "Thou suffering thing,
Know that thy sorrow is my ecstasy,
That thy love's loss is my hate's profiting!"

Then would I bear it, clench myself, and die,
Steeled by the sense of ire unmerited;
Half-eased in that a Powerfuller than I
Had willed and meted me the tears I shed.

But not so. How arrives it joy lies slain,
And why unblooms the best hope ever sown?
—Crass Casualty obstructs the sun and rain,
And dicing Time for gladness casts a moan. . . .
These purblind Doomsters had as readily strown
Blisses about my pilgrimage as pain.

She, to Him (I)

When you shall see me in the toils of Time,
My lauded beauties carried off from me,
My eyes no longer stars as in their prime,
My name forgot of Maiden Fair and Free;

When in your being heart concedes to mind,
And judgement, though you scarce its process know,
Recalls the excellences I once enshrined,
And you are irk'd that they have wither'd so;

Remembering mine the loss is, not the blame,
That Sportsman Time but rears his brood to kill,
Knowing me in my soul the very same—
One who would die to spare you touch of ill!—
Will you not grant to old affection's claim
The hand of friendship down Life's sunless hill?

At a Lunar Eclipse

Thy shadow, Earth, from Pole to Central Sea,
Now steals along upon the Moon's meek shine
In even monochrome and curving line
Of imperturbable serenity.

How shall I link such sun-cast symmetry
With the torn troubled form I know as thine,
That profile, placid as a brow divine,
With continents of moil and misery?

And can immense Mortality but throw
So small a shade, and Heaven's high human scheme
Be hemmed within the coasts yon arc implies?

Is such the stellar gauge of earthly show,
Nation at war with nation, brains that teem,
Heroes, and women fairer than the skies?

A Church Romance

She turned in the high pew, until her sight
Swept the west gallery, and caught its row
Of music-men with viol, book, and bow
Against the sinking sad tower-window light.

She turned again; and in her pride's despite
One strenuous viol's inspirer seemed to throw
A message from his string to her below,
Which said: "I claim thee as my own forthright!"

Thus their hearts' bond began, in due time signed.
And long years thence, when Age had scared Romance,
At some old attitude of his or glance
That gallery-scene would break upon her mind,
With him as minstrel, ardent, young, and trim,
Bowing "New Sabbath" or "Mount Ephraim."

Over the Coffin

They stand confronting, the coffin between,
His wife of old, and his wife of late,
And the dead man whose they both had been
Seems listening aloof, as to things past date.
—"I have called," says the first. "Do you marvel or not?"
"In truth," says the second, "I do—somewhat."

"Well, there was a word to be said by me! . . .
I divorced that man because of you—
It seemed I must do it, boundenly;
But now I am older, and tell you true,
For life is little, and dead lies he;
I would I had let alone you two!
And both of us, scorning parochial ways,
Had lived like the wives in the patriarchs' days."

We Are Getting to the End

We are getting to the end of visioning
The impossible within this universe,
Such as that better whiles may follow worse,
And that our race may mend by reasoning.

We know that even as larks in cages sing
Unthoughtful of deliverance from the curse
That holds them lifelong in a latticed hearse,
We ply spasmodically our pleasuring.

And that when nations set them to lay waste
Their neighbours' heritage by foot and horse,
And hack their pleasant plains in festering seams,
They may again,—not warely, or from taste,
But tickled mad by some demonic force.—
Yes. We are getting to the end of dreams!

ROBERT BRIDGES

"While yet we wait for spring, and from the dry"

While yet we wait for spring, and from the dry
And blackening east that so embitters March,
Well-housed must watch grey fields and meadows parch,
And driven dust and withering snowflake fly;
Already in glimpses of the tarnish'd sky
The sun is warm and beckons to the larch,
And where the covert hazels interarch
Their tassell'd twigs, fair beds of primrose lie.

Beneath the crisp and wintry carpet hid
A million buds but stay their blossoming;
And trustful birds have built their nests amid
The shuddering boughs, and only wait to sing
Till one soft shower from the south shall bid,
And hither tempt the pilgrim steps of spring.

GERARD MANLEY HOPKINS

God's Grandeur

The world is charged with the grandeur of God.
    It will flame out, like shining from shook foil;
    It gathers to a greatness, like the ooze of oil
Crushed. Why do men then now not reck his rod?
Generations have trod, have trod, have trod;
    And all is seared with trade; bleared, smeared with toil;
    And wears man's smudge and shares man's smell: the soil
Is bare now, nor can foot feel, being shod.

And for all this, nature is never spent;
    There lives the dearest freshness deep down things;
And though the last lights off the black West went
    Oh, morning, at the brown brink eastward, springs—
Because the Holy Ghost over the bent
    World broods with warm breast and with ah! bright wings.

"As kingfishers catch fire, dragonflies draw flame"

As kingfishers catch fire, dragonflies draw flame;
    As tumbled over rim in roundy wells
    Stones ring; like each tucked string tells, each hung bell's
Bow swung finds tongue to fling out broad its name;
Each mortal thing does one thing and the same:
    Deals out that being indoors each one dwells;
    Selves—goes its self; *myself* it speaks and spells,
Crying *What I do is me; for that I came.*

I say more: the just man justices;
    Keeps grace: that keeps all his goings graces;
Acts in God's eye what in God's eye he is—
    Christ. For Christ plays in ten thousand places,
Lovely in limbs, and lovely in eyes not his
    To the Father through the features of men's faces.

Spring

Nothing is so beautiful as Spring—
    When weeds, in wheels, shoot long and lovely and lush;
    Thrush's eggs look little low heavens, and thrush
Through the echoing timber does so rinse and wring
The ear, it strikes like lightnings to hear him sing;
    The glassy peartree leaves and blooms, they brush
    The descending blue; that blue is all in a rush
With richness; the racing lambs too have fair their fling.

What is all this juice and all this joy?
    A strain of the earth's sweet being in the beginning
In Eden's garden.—Have, get before it cloy,
    Before it cloud, Christ, lord, and sour with sinning,
Innocent mind and Mayday in girl and boy,
    Most, O maid's child, thy choice and worthy the winning.

The Windhover
To Christ our Lord

I caught this morning morning's minion, king-
    dom of daylight's dauphin, dapple-dáwn-drawn Falcon, in his
        riding
    Of the rólling level úndernéath him steady áir, and stríding
High there, how he rung upon the rein of a wimpling wing
In his ecstasy! then off, off forth on swing,
    As a skate's heel sweeps smooth on a bow-bend: the hurl and
        gliding
    Rebuffed the big wind. My heart in hiding
Stirred for a bird,—the achieve of, the mastery of the thing!

Brute beauty and valour and act, oh, air, pride, plume, here
    Buckle! AND the fire that breaks from thee then, a billion
Times told lovelier, more dangerous, O my chevalier!

    No wónder of it: shéer plód makes plóugh down síllion
Shine, and blue-bleak embers, ah my dear,
    Fall, gáll themsélves, and gásh góld-vermílion.

Pied Beauty

Glory be to God for dappled things—
    For skies of couple-colour as a brinded cow;
      For rose-moles all in stipple upon trout that swim;
Fresh-firecoal chestnut-falls; finches' wings;
    Landscape plotted and pieced—fold, fallow, and plough;
    And áll trades, their gear and tackle and trim.

All things counter, original, spáre, strange;
    Whatever is fickle, frecklèd (who knows how?)
      With swíft, slów; sweet, sóur; adázzle, dím;
He fathers-forth whose beauty is pást change:
                    Práise hím.

Felix Randal

Félix Rándal the fárrier, O is he déad then? my dúty all énded,
Who have watched his mould of man, big-boned and
    hardy-handsome
Pining, pining, till time when reason rambled in it and some
Fatal four disorders, fleshed there, all contended?

Sickness broke him. Impatient, he cursed at first, but mended
Being anointed and all; though a heavenlier heart began some
Mónths éarlier, since I had our swéet repriéve and ránsom
Téndered to him. Áh well, God rést him áll road éver he offénded!

This séeing the síck endéars them tó us, us tóo it endéars.
My tongue had taught thee comfort, touch had quenched thy
    tears,
Thy tears that touched my heart, child, Felix, poor Felix Randal;

How far from then forethought of, all thy more boisterous years,
When thou at the random grim forge, powerful amidst peers,
Didst fettle for the great grey drayhorse his bright and battering
    sandal!

"I wake and feel the fell of dark, not day"

I wake and feel the fell of dark, not day.
What hours, O what black hours we have spent
This night! what sights you, heart, saw; ways you went!
And more must, in yet longer light's delay.

With witness I speak this. But where I say
Hours I mean years, mean life. And my lament
Is cries countless, cries like dead letters sent
To dearest him that lives alas! away.

I am gall, I am heartburn. God's most deep decree
Bitter would have me taste: my taste was me;
Bones built in me, flesh filled, blood brimmed the curse.

Selfyeast of spirit a dull dough sours. I see
The lost are like this, and their scourge to be
As I am mine, their sweating selves; but worse.

"No worst, there is none. Pitched past pitch of grief"

No worst, there is none. Pitched past pitch of grief,
More pangs will, schooled at forepangs, wilder wring.
Comforter, where, where is your comforting?
Mary, mother of us, where is your relief?
My cries heave, herds-long; huddle in a main, a chief-
Woe, wórld-sorrow; on an áge-old ánvil wínce and síng—
Then lull, then leave off. Fury had shrieked "No ling-
Ering! Let me be fell: force I must be brief."
O the mind, mind has mountains; cliffs of fall
Frightful, sheer, no-man-fathomed. Hold them cheap
May who ne'er hung there. Nor does long our small
Durance deal with that steep or deep. Here! creep,
Wretch, under a comfort serves in a whirlwind: all
Life death does and each day dies with sleep.

That Nature is a Heraclitean Fire and of the Comfort of the Resurrection

Cloud-puffball, torn tufts, tossed pillows | flaunt forth, then chevy on an air-
Built thoroughfare: heaven-roysterers, in gay-gangs | they throng; they glitter in marches.
Down roughcast, down dazzling whitewash, | wherever an elm arches,
Shivelights and shadowtackle in long | lashes lace, lance, and pair.
Delightfully the bright wind boisterous | ropes, wrestles, beats earth bare
Of yestertempest's creases; in pool and rutpeel parches
Squandering ooze to squeezed | dough, crust, dust; stanches, starches
Squadroned masks and manmarks | treadmire toil there
Footfretted in it. Million-fuèled, | nature's bonfire burns on.
But quench her bonniest, dearest | to her, her clearest-selvèd spark
Man, how fast his firedint, | his mark on mind, is gone!
Both are in an únfathomable, all is in an enormous dark
Drowned. O pity an indig | nation! Manshape, that shone
Sheer off, disseveral, a star, | death blots black out; nor mark
              Is any of him at all so stark
But vastness blurs and time | beats level. Enough! The Resurrection,
A heart's-clarion! Away grief 's gasping, | joyless days, dejection.
              Across my foundering deck shone
A beacon, an eternal beam. | Flesh fade, and mortal trash
Fall to the residuary worm; | world's wildfire, leave but ash:
              In a flash, at a trumpet crash,
I am all at once what Christ is, | since he was what I am, and
This Jack, joke, poor potsherd, | patch, matchwood, immortal diamond,
              Is immortal diamond.

"Thou art indeed just, Lord, if I contend"

*Justus quidem tu es, Domine, si disputem tecum; verumtamen justa
loquar ad te: Quare via impiorum prosperatur? &c (Jerem. xii I.)*

Thou art indeed just, Lord, if I contend
With thee; but, sir, so what I plead is just.
Why do sinners' ways prosper? and why must
Disappointment all I endeavour end?

Wert thou my enemy, O thou my friend,
How wouldst thou worse, I wonder, than thou dost
Defeat, thwart me? Oh, the sots and thralls of lust
Do in spare hours more thrive than I that spend,

Sir, life upon thy cause. See, banks and brakes
Now, leavèd how thick! lacèd they are again
With fretty chervil, look, and fresh wind shakes

Them; birds build—but not I build; no, but strain,
Time's eunuch, and not breed one work that wakes.
Mine, O thou lord of life, send my roots rain.

EMMA LAZARUS

The New Colossus

Not like the brazen giant of Greek fame,
With conquering limbs astride from land to land,
Here at our sea-washed, sunset-gates shall stand
A mighty woman with a torch, whose flame
Is the imprisoned lightning, and her name
Mother of Exiles. From her beacon-hand
Glows world-wide welcome, her mild eyes command
The air-bridged harbor that twin-cities frame.
"Keep, ancient lands, your storied pomp!" cries she,
With silent lips. "Give me your tired, your poor,
Your huddled masses yearning to breathe free,
The wretched refuse of your teeming shore,
Send these, the homeless, tempest-tost to me,
I lift my lamp beside the golden door!"

OSCAR WILDE

Hélas

To drift with every passion till my soul
Is a stringed lute on which all winds can play,
Is it for this that I have given away
Mine ancient wisdom, and austere control?
Methinks my life is a twice-written scroll
Scrawled over on some boyish holiday
With idle songs for pipe and virelay,
Which do but mar the secret of the whole.
Surely there was a time I might have trod
The sunlit heights, and from life's dissonance
Struck one clear chord to reach the ears of God.
Is that time dead? lo! with a little rod
I did but touch the honey of romance—
And must I lose a soul's inheritance?

W. B. YEATS

The Folly of Being Comforted

One that is ever kind said yesterday:
"Your well-belovèd's hair has threads of grey,
And little shadows come about her eyes;
Time can but make it easier to be wise
Though now it seem impossible, and so
All that you need is patience."

                    Heart cries, "No,
I have not a crumb of comfort, not a grain.
Time can but make her beauty over again:
Because of that great nobleness of hers
The fire that stirs about her, when she stirs,
Burns but more clearly. O she had not these ways
When all the wild summer was in her gaze."

O heart! O heart! if she'd but turn her head,
You'd know the folly of being comforted.

The Fascination of What's Difficult

The fascination of what's difficult
Has dried the sap out of my veins, and rent
Spontaneous joy and natural content
Out of my heart. There's something ails our colt
That must, as if it had not holy blood
Nor on Olympus leaped from cloud to cloud,
Shiver under the lash, strain, sweat and jolt
As though it dragged road-metal. My curse on plays
That have to be set up in fifty ways,
On the day's war with every knave and dolt,
Theatre business, management of men.
I swear before the dawn comes round again
I'll find the stable and pull out the bolt.

At the Abbey Theatre
(Imitated from Ronsard)

Dear Craoibhin Aoibhin, look into our case.
When we are high and airy hundreds say
That if we hold that flight they'll leave the place,
While those same hundreds mock another day
Because we have made our art of common things,
So bitterly, you'd dream they longed to look
All their lives through into some drift of wings.
You've dandled them and fed them from the book
And know them to the bone; impart to us—
We'll keep the secret—a new trick to please.
Is there a bridle for this Proteus
That turns and changes like his draughty seas?
Or is there none, most popular of men,
But when they mock us, that we mock again?

Leda and the Swan

A sudden blow; the great wings beating still
Above the staggering girl, her thighs caressed
By the dark webs, her nape caught in his bill,
He holds her helpless breast upon his breast.

How can those terrified vague fingers push
The feathered glory from her loosening thighs?
And how can body, laid in that white rush,
But feel the strange heart beating where it lies?

A shudder in the loins engenders there
The broken wall, the burning roof and tower
And Agamemnon dead.
                      Being so caught up,
So mastered by the brute blood of the air,
Did she put on his knowledge with his power
Before the indifferent beak could let her drop?

Meru

Civilisation is hooped together, brought
Under a rule, under the semblance of peace
By manifold illusion; but man's life is thought,
And he, despite his terror, cannot cease
Ravening through century after century,
Ravening, raging, and uprooting that he may come
Into the desolation of reality:
Egypt and Greece, good-bye, and good-bye, Rome!
Hermits upon Mount Meru or Everest,
Caverned in night under the drifted snow,
Or where that snow and winter's dreadful blast
Beat down upon their naked bodies, know
That day brings round the night, that before dawn
His glory and his monuments are gone.

ERNEST DOWSON

A Last Word

Let us go hence: the night is now at hand;
The day is overworn, the birds all flown;
And we have reaped the crops the gods have sown;
Despair and death; deep darkness o'er the land,
Broods like an owl; we cannot understand
Laughter or tears, for we have only known
Surpassing vanity: vain things alone
Have driven our perverse and aimless band.
Let us go hence, somewhither strange and cold,
To Hollow Lands where just men and unjust
Find end of labour, where's rest for the old,
Freedom to all from love and fear and lust.
Twine our torn hands! O pray the earth enfold
Our life-sick hearts and turn them into dust.

EDWARD ARLINGTON ROBINSON

Firelight

Ten years together without yet a cloud,
They seek each other's eyes at intervals
Of gratefulness to firelight and four walls
For love's obliteration of the crowd.
Serenely and perennially endowed
And bowered as few may be, their joy recalls
No snake, no sword, and over them there falls
The blessing of what neither says aloud.

Wiser for silence, they were not so glad
Were she to read the graven tale of lines
On the wan face of one somewhere alone;
Nor were they more content could he have had
Her thoughts a moment since of one who shines
Apart, and would be hers if he had known.

Cliff Klingenhagen

Cliff Klingenhagen had me in to dine
With him one day; and after soup and meat,
And all the other things there were to eat,
Cliff took two glasses and filled one with wine
And one with wormwood. Then, without a sign
For me to choose at all, he took the draught
Of bitterness himself, and lightly quaffed
It off, and said the other one was mine.

And when I asked him what the deuce he meant
By doing that, he only looked at me
And smiled, and said it was a way of his.
And though I know the fellow, I have spent
Long time a-wondering when I shall be
As happy as Cliff Klingenhagen is.

Reuben Bright

Because he was a butcher and thereby
Did earn an honest living (and did right),
I would not have you think that Reuben Bright
Was any more a brute than you or I;
For when they told him that his wife must die,
He stared at them, and shook with grief and fright,
And cried like a great baby half that night,
And made the women cry to see him cry.

And after she was dead, and he had paid
The singers and the sexton and the rest,
He packed a lot of things that she had made
Most mournfully away in an old chest
Of hers, and put some chopped-up cedar boughs
In with them, and tore down the slaughter house.

The Sheaves

Where long the shadows of the wind had rolled,
Green wheat was yielding to the change assigned;
And as by some vast magic undivined
The world was turning slowly into gold.
Like nothing that was ever bought or sold
It waited there, the body and the mind;
And with a mighty meaning of a kind
That tells the more the more it is not told.

So in a land where all days are not fair,
Fair days went on till on another day
A thousand golden sheaves were lying there,
Shining and still, but not for long to stay—
As if a thousand girls with golden hair
Might rise from where they slept and go away.

TRUMBULL STICKNEY

"Be still. The Hanging Gardens were a dream"

Be still. The Hanging Gardens were a dream
That over Persian roses flew to kiss
The curled lashes of Semiramis.
Troy never was, nor green Skamander stream.
Provence and Troubadour are merest lies,
The glorious hair of Venice was a beam
Made with Titian's eye. The sunsets seem,
The world is very old and nothing is.
Be still. Thou foolish thing, thou canst not wake,
Nor thy tears wedge thy soldered lids apart,
But patter in the darkness of thy heart.
Thy brain is plagued. Thou art a frightened owl
Blind with the light of life thou'ldst not forsake,
And error loves and nourishes thy soul.

Six O'Clock

Now burst above the city's cold twilight
The piercing whistles and the tower-clocks:
For day is done. Along the frozen docks
The workmen set their ragged shirts aright.
Thro' factory doors a stream of dingy light
Follows the scrimmage as it quickly flocks
To hut and home among the snow's gray blocks.—
I love you, human labourers. Good-night!
Good-night to all the blackened arms that ache!
Good-night to every sick and sweated brow,
To the poor girl that strength and love forsake,
To the poor boy who can no more! I vow
The victim soon shall shudder at the stake
And fall in blood: we bring him even now.

RUPERT BROOKE

The Hill

Breathless, we flung us on the windy hill,
　　Laughed in the sun, and kissed the lovely grass.
　　You said, "Through glory and ecstasy we pass;
Wind, sun, and earth remain, the birds sing still,
When we are old, are old. . . ." "And when we die
　　All's over that is ours; and life burns on
Through other lovers, other lips," said I,
　　"Heart of my heart, our heaven is now, is won!"

"We are Earth's best, that learnt her lesson here.
　　Life is our cry. We have kept the faith!" we said;
　　"We shall go down with unreluctant tread
Rose-crowned into the darkness!" . . . Proud we were,
And laughed, that had such brave true things to say.
—And then you suddenly cried, and turned away.

Clouds

Down the blue night the unending columns press
In noiseless tumult, break and wave and flow,
Now tread the far South, or lift rounds of snow
Up to the white moon's hidden loveliness.
Some pause in their grave wandering comradeless,
And turn with profound gesture vague and slow,
As who would pray good for the world, but know
Their benediction empty as they bless.

They say that the Dead die not, but remain
Near to the rich heirs of their grief and mirth.
I think they ride the calm mid-heaven, as these,
In wise majestic melancholy train,
And watch the moon, and the still-raging seas,
And men, coming and going on the earth.

A Memory

Somewhile before the dawn I rose, and stept
Softly along the dim way to your room,
And found you sleeping in the quiet gloom,
And holiness about you as you slept.
I knelt there; till your waking fingers crept
About my head, and held it. I had rest
Unhoped this side of Heaven, beneath your breast.
I knelt a long time, still; nor even wept.

It was great wrong you did me; and for gain
Of that poor moment's kindliness, and ease,
And sleepy mother-comfort!
                                        Child, you know
How easily love leaps out to dreams like these,
Who has seen them true. And love that's wakened so
Takes all too long to lay asleep again.

The Soldier

If I should die, think only this of me;
    That there's some corner of a foreign field
That is for ever England. There shall be
    In that rich earth a richer dust concealed;
A dust whom England bore, shaped, made aware,
    Gave, once, her flowers to love, her ways to roam,
A body of England's breathing English air,
    Washed by the rivers, blessed by suns of home.

And think, this heart, all evil shed away,
    A pulse in the eternal mind, no less
        Gives somewhere back the thoughts by England given;
Her sights and sounds; dreams happy as her day;
    And laughter, learned of friends; and gentleness,
        In hearts at peace, under an English heaven.

ALICE DUNBAR-NELSON

Sonnet

I had no thought of violets of late,
The wild, shy kind that spring beneath your feet
In wistful April days, when lovers mate
And wander through the fields in raptures sweet.
The thought of violets meant florists' shops,
And bows and pins, and perfumed papers fine;
And garish lights, and mincing little fops
And cabarets and songs, and deadening wine.
So far from sweet real things my thoughts had strayed,
I had forgot wide fields, and clear brown streams;
The perfect loveliness that God has made,—
Wild violets shy and Heaven-mounting dreams.
And now—unwittingly, you've made me dream
Of violets, and my soul's forgotten gleam.

ROBERT FROST

A Dream Pang

I had withdrawn in forest, and my song
Was swallowed up in leaves that blew away;
And to the forest edge you came one day
(This was my dream) and looked and pondered long,
But did not enter, though the wish was strong:
You shook your pensive head as who should say,
"I dare not—too far in his footsteps stray—
He must seek me would he undo the wrong."

Not far, but near, I stood and saw it all,
Behind low boughs the trees let down outside;
And the sweet pang it cost me not to call
And tell you that I saw does still abide.
But 'tis not true that thus I dwelt aloof,
For the wood wakes, and you are here for proof.

Hyla Brook

By June our brook's run out of song and speed.
Sought for much after that, it will be found
Either to have gone groping underground
(And taken with it all the Hyla breed
That shouted in the mist a month ago,
Like ghost of sleigh bells in a ghost of snow)—
Or flourished and come up in jewelweed,
Weak foliage that is blown upon and bent,
Even against the way its waters went.
Its bed is left a faded paper sheet
Of dead leaves stuck together by the heat—
A brook to none but who remember long.
This as it will be seen is other far
Than with brooks taken otherwhere in song.
We love the things we love for what they are.

The Oven Bird

There is a singer everyone has heard,
Loud, a mid-summer and a mid-wood bird,
Who makes the solid tree trunks sound again.
He says that leaves are old and that for flowers
Mid-summer is to spring as one to ten.
He says the early petal-fall is past,
When pear and cherry bloom went down in showers
On sunny days a moment overcast;
And comes that other fall we name the fall.
He says the highway dust is over all.
The bird would cease and be as other birds
But that he knows in singing not to sing.
The question that he frames in all but words
Is what to make of a diminished thing.

Range-Finding

The battle rent a cobweb diamond-strung
And cut a flower beside a groundbird's nest
Before it stained a single human breast.
The stricken flower bent double and so hung.
And still the bird revisited her young.
A butterfly its fall had dispossessed,
A moment sought in air his flower of rest,
Then lightly stooped to it and fluttering clung.
On the bare upland pasture there had spread
O'ernight 'twixt mullein stalks a wheel of thread
And straining cables wet with silver dew.
A sudden passing bullet shook it dry.
The indwelling spider ran to greet the fly,
But finding nothing, sullenly withdrew.

Acquainted with the Night

I have been one acquainted with the night.
I have walked out in rain—and back in rain.
I have outwalked the furthest city light.

I have looked down the saddest city lane.
I have passed by the watchman on his beat
And dropped my eyes, unwilling to explain.

I have stood still and stopped the sound of feet
When far away an interrupted cry
Came over houses from another street,

But not to call me back or say good-by;
And further still at an unearthly height
One luminary clock against the sky

Proclaimed the time was neither wrong nor right.
I have been one acquainted with the night.

Design

I found a dimpled spider, fat and white,
On a white heal-all, holding up a moth
Like a white piece of rigid satin cloth—
Assorted characters of death and blight
Mixed ready to begin the morning right,
Like the ingredients of a witches' broth—
A snow-drop spider, a flower like a froth,
And dead wings carried like a paper kite.

What had that flower to do with being white,
The wayside blue and innocent heal-all?
What brought the kindred spider to that height,
Then steered the white moth thither in the night?
What but design of darkness to appall?—
If design govern in a thing so small.

The Silken Tent

She is as in a field a silken tent
At midday when a sunny summer breeze
Has dried the dew and all its ropes relent,
So that in guys it gently sways at ease,
And its supporting central cedar pole,
That is its pinnacle to heavenward
And signifies the sureness of the soul,
Seems to owe naught to any single cord,
But strictly held by none, is loosely bound
By countless silken ties of love and thought
To everything on earth the compass round,
And only by one's going slightly taut
In the capriciousness of summer air
Is of the slightest bondage made aware.

Never Again Would Birds' Song Be the Same

He would declare and could himself believe
That the birds there in all the garden round
From having heard the daylong voice of Eve
Had added to their own an oversound,
Her tone of meaning but without the words.
Admittedly an eloquence so soft
Could only have had an influence on birds
When call or laughter carried it aloft.
Be that as may be, she was in their song.
Moreover her voice upon their voices crossed
Had now persisted in the woods so long
That probably it never would be lost.
Never again would birds' song be the same.
And to do that to birds was why she came.

EDWARD THOMAS

Some Eyes Condemn

Some eyes condemn the earth they gaze upon:
Some wait patiently till they know far more
Than earth can tell them: some laugh at the whole
As folly of another's making: one
I knew that laughed because he saw, from core
To rind, not one thing worth the laugh his soul
Had ready at waking: some eyes have begun
With laughing; some stand startled at the door.

Others, too, I have seen rest, question, roll,
Dance, shoot. And many I have loved watching. Some
I could not take my eyes from till they turned
And loving died. I had not found my goal.
But thinking of your eyes, dear, I become
Dumb: for they flamed and it was me they burned.

February Afternoon

Men heard this roar of parleying starlings, saw,
    A thousand years ago even as now,
    Black rooks with white gulls following the plough
So that the first are last until a caw
Commands that last are first again,—a law
    Which was of old when one, like me, dreamed how
    A thousand years might dust lie on his brow
Yet thus would birds do between hedge and shaw.

Time swims before me, making as a day
    A thousand years, while the broad ploughland oak
    Roars mill-like and men strike and bear the stroke
    Of war as ever, audacious or resigned,
And God still sits aloft in the array
    That we have wrought him, stone-deaf and stone-blind.

EZRA POUND

A Virginal

No, no! Go from me. I have left her lately,
I will not spoil my sheath with lesser brightness,
For my surrounding air hath a new lightness;
Slight are her arms, yet they have bound me straitly
And left me cloaked as with a gauze of ether;
As with sweet leaves; as with subtle clearness.
Oh, I have picked up magic in her nearness
To sheathe me half in half the things that sheathe her.
No, no! Go from me. I have still the flavor,
Soft as spring wind that's come from birchen bowers.
Green come the shoots, aye April in the branches,
As winter's wound with her sleight hand she staunches,
Hath of the trees a likeness of the savor:
As white their bark, so white this lady's hours.

ELINOR WYLIE

Sonnet

When, in the dear beginning of the fever
Whose one remedial physic must be death,
I drew the light and unembittered breath
Of ecstasy, then was I brave and clever;
No pinch of dust presumed to whisper "never";
The soul had exorcised the body's wraith,
In sacred madness and severer faith,
And this delirium should endure forever.

Then was my throat obedient as a reed
Wherein a demigod is audible;
But now its stops are practised to foretell
Only the mortal doom, the murderous deed:
Yet, if my love is pleased to whistle once,
The silver still cries out above the bronze.

A Lodging for the Night

If I had lightly given at the first
The lightest favours that you first demanded;
Had I been prodigal and open-handed
Of this dead body in its dream immersed;
My flesh and not my spirit had been pierced:
Your appetite was casual and candid;
Thus, for an hour, had endured and ended
My love, in violation and reversed.

Alas, because I would not draw the bolt
And take you to my bed, you now assume
The likeness of an angel in revolt
Turned from a low inhospitable room,
Until your fiery image has enchanted
And ravished the poor soul you never wanted.

SIEGFRIED SASSOON

Dreamers

Soldiers are citizens of death's grey land,
     Drawing no dividend from time's tomorrows.
In the great hour of destiny they stand,
     Each with his feuds, and jealousies, and sorrows.

Soldiers are sworn to action; they must win
     Some flaming, fatal climax with their lives.
Soldiers are dreamers, when the guns begin
     They think of firelit homes, clean beds, and wives.

I see them in foul dug-outs, gnawed by rats,
     And in the ruined trenches, lashed with rain,
Dreaming of things they did with balls and bats,
     And mocked by hopeless longing to regain
Bank-holidays, and picture shows, and spats,
     And going to the office in the train.

Glory of Women

You love us when we're heroes, home on leave,
Or wounded in a mentionable place.
You worship decorations; you believe
That chivalry redeems the war's disgrace.
You make us shells. You listen with delight,
By tales of dirt and danger fondly thrilled.
You crown our distant ardours while we fight,
And mourn our laurelled memories when we're killed.
You can't believe that British troops "retire"
When hell's last horror breaks them, and they run,
Trampling the terrible corpses—blind with blood.
 O German mother dreaming by the fire,
While you are knitting socks to send your son
His face is trodden deeper in the mud.

On Passing the New Menin Gate

Who will remember, passing through this Gate,
The unheroic Dead who fed the guns?
Who shall absolve the foulness of their fate,—
Those doomed, conscripted, unvictorious ones?
 Crudely renewed, the Salient holds its own.
 Paid are its dim defenders by this pomp;
 Paid, with a pile of peace-complacent stone,
 The armies who endured that sullen swamp.

Here was the world's worst wound. And here with pride
"Their name liveth for ever," the Gateway claims.
Was ever an immolation so belied
As these intolerably nameless names?
Well might the Dead who struggled in the slime
Rise and deride this sepulchre of crime.

ROBINSON JEFFERS

Love the Wild Swan

"I hate my verses, every line, every word.
Oh pale and brittle pencils ever to try
One grass-blade's curve, or the throat of one bird
That clings to twig, ruffled against white sky.
Oh cracked and twilight mirrors ever to catch
One color, one glinting flash, of the splendor of things.
Unlucky hunter, Oh bullets of wax,
The lion beauty, the wild-swan wings, the storm of the wings."
—This wild swan of a world is no hunter's game.
Better bullets than yours would miss the white breast,
Better mirrors than yours would crack in the flame.
Does it matter whether you hate your . . . self? At least
Love your eyes that can see, your mind that can
Hear the music, the thunder of the wings. Love the wild swan.

MARIANNE MOORE

No Swan So Fine

"No water so still as the
      dead fountains of Versailles." No swan,
with swart blind look askance
and gondoliering legs, so fine
      as the chintz china one with fawn-
brown eyes and toothed gold
collar on to show whose bird it was.

Lodged in the Louis Fifteenth
      candelabrum-tree of cockscomb-
tinted buttons, dahlias,
sea-urchins, and everlastings,
      it perches on the branching foam
of polished sculptured
flowers—at ease and tall. The king is dead.

EDWIN MUIR

Milton

Milton, his face set fair for Paradise,
And knowing that he and Paradise were lost
In separate desolation, bravely crossed
Into his second night and paid his price.
There towards the end he to the dark tower came
Set square in the gate, a mass of blackened stone
Crowned with vermilion fiends like streamers blown
From a great funnel filled with roaring flame.

Shut in his darkness, these he could not see,
But heard the steely clamour known too well
On Saturday nights in every street in Hell.
Where, past the devilish din, could Paradise be?
A footstep more, and his unblinded eyes
Saw far and near the fields of Paradise.

T. S. ELIOT

from *The Dry Salvages* [Section I, opening stanza]

I do not know much about gods; but I think that the river
Is a strong brown god—sullen, untamed and intractable,
Patient to some degree, at first recognised as a frontier;
Useful, untrustworthy, as a conveyor of commerce;
Then only a problem confronting the builder of bridges.
The problem once solved, the brown god is almost forgotten
By the dwellers in cities—ever, however, implacable,
Keeping his seasons and rages, destroyer, reminder
Of what men choose to forget. Unhonoured, unpropitiated
By worshippers of the machine, but waiting, watching and waiting.
His rhythm was present in the nursery bedroom,
In the rank ailanthus of the April dooryard,
In the smell of grapes on the autumn table,
And the evening circle in the winter gaslight.

JOHN CROWE RANSOM

Piazza Piece

—I am a gentleman in a dustcoat trying
To make you hear. Your ears are soft and small
And listen to an old man not at all,
They want the young men's whispering and sighing.
But see the roses on your trellis dying
And hear the spectral singing of the moon;
For I must have my lovely lady soon,
I am a gentleman in a dustcoat trying.

—I am a lady young in beauty waiting
Until my truelove comes, and then we kiss.
But what grey man among the vines is this
Whose words are dry and faint as in a dream?
Back from my trellis, Sir, before I scream!
I am a lady young in beauty waiting.

CLAUDE McKAY

If We Must Die

If we must die, let it not be like hogs
Hunted and penned in an inglorious spot,
While round us bark the mad and hungry dogs,
Making their mock at our accursed lot.
If we must die, O let us nobly die,
So that our precious blood may not be shed
In vain; then even the monsters we defy
Shall be constrained to honor us though dead!
O kinsmen! we must meet the common foe!
Though far outnumbered let us show us brave,
And for their thousand blows deal one deathblow!
What though before us lies the open grave?
Like men we'll face the murderous, cowardly pack,
Pressed to the wall, dying, but fighting back!

America

Although she feeds me bread of bitterness,
And sinks into my throat her tiger's tooth,
Stealing my breath of life, I will confess
I love this cultured hell that tests my youth!
Her vigor flows like tides into my blood,
Giving me strength erect against her hate.
Her bigness sweeps my being like a flood.
Yet as a rebel fronts a king in state,
I stand within her walls with not a shred
Of terror, malice, not a word of jeer.
Darkly I gaze into the days ahead,
And see her might and granite wonders there,
Beneath the touch of time's unerring hand,
Like priceless treasures sinking in the sand.

ARCHIBALD MacLEISH

The End of the World

Quite unexpectedly as Vasserot
The armless ambidextrian was lighting
A match between his great and second toe
And Ralph the lion was engaged in biting
The neck of Madame Sossman while the drum
Pointed, and Teeny was about to cough
In waltz time swinging Jocko by the thumb—
Quite unexpectedly the top blew off:

And there, there overhead, there, there, hung over
Those thousands of white faces, those dazed eyes,
There in the starless dark the poise, the hover,
There with vast wings across the canceled skies,
There in the sudden blackness the black pall
Of nothing, nothing, nothing—nothing at all.

EDNA ST. VINCENT MILLAY

"If I should learn, in some quite casual way"

If I should learn, in some quite casual way,
That you were gone, not to return again—
Read from the back-page of a paper, say,
Held by a neighbor in a subway train,
How at the corner of this avenue
And such a street (so are the papers filled)
A hurrying man, who happened to be you,
At noon today had happened to be killed,
I should not cry aloud—I could not cry
Aloud, or wring my hands in such a place—
I should but watch the station lights rush by
With a more careful interest on my face;
Or raise my eyes and read with greater care
Where to store furs and how to treat the hair.

"Pity me not because the light of day"

Pity me not because the light of day
At close of day no longer walks the sky;
Pity me not for beauties passed away
From field and thicket as the year goes by;
Pity me not the waning of the moon,
Nor that the ebbing tide goes out to sea,
Nor that a man's desire is hushed so soon,
And you no longer look with love on me.
This have I known always: Love is no more
Than the wide blossom which the wind assails,
Than the great tide that treads the shifting shore,
Strewing fresh wreckage gathered in the gales:
Pity me that the heart is slow to learn
What the swift mind beholds at every turn.

"I shall go back again to the bleak shore"

I shall go back again to the bleak shore
And build a little shanty on the sand,
In such a way that the extremest band
Of brittle seaweed will escape my door
But by a yard or two; and nevermore
Shall I return to take you by the hand;
I shall be gone to what I understand,
And happier than I ever was before.
The love that stood a moment in your eyes,
The words that lay a moment on your tongue,
Are one with all that in a moment dies,
A little under-said and over-sung.
But I shall find the sullen rocks and skies
Unchanged from what they were when I was young.

"I, being born a woman and distressed"

I, being born a woman and distressed
By all the needs and notions of my kind,
Am urged by your propinquity to find
Your person fair, and feel a certain zest
To bear your body's weight upon my breast:
So subtly is the fume of life designed,
To clarify the pulse and cloud the mind,
And leave me once again undone, possessed.
Think not for this, however, the poor treason
Of my stout blood against my staggering brain,
I shall remember you with love, or season
My scorn with pity,—let me make it plain:
I find this frenzy insufficient reason
For conversation when we meet again.

"What lips my lips have kissed, and where, and why"

What lips my lips have kissed, and where, and why,
I have forgotten, and what arms have lain
Under my head till morning; but the rain
Is full of ghosts tonight, that tap and sigh
Upon the glass and listen for reply,
And in my heart there stirs a quiet pain
For unremembered lads that not again
Will turn to me at midnight with a cry.
Thus in the winter stands the lonely tree,
Nor knows what birds have vanished one by one,
Yet knows its boughs more silent than before:
I cannot say what loves have come and gone,
I only know that summer sang in me
A little while, that in me sings no more.

from *Fatal Interview*

II

This beast that rends me in the sight of all,
This love, this longing, this oblivious thing,
That has me under as the last leaves fall,
Will glut, will sicken, will be gone by spring.
The wound will heal, the fever will abate,
The knotted hurt will slacken in the breast;
I shall forget before the flickers mate
Your look that is today my east and west.
Unscathed, however, from a claw so deep
Though I should love again I shall not go:
Along my body, waking while I sleep,
Sharp to the kiss, cold to the hand as snow,
The scar of this encounter like a sword
Will lie between me and my troubled lord.

VII

Night is my sister, and how deep in love,
How drowned in love and weedily washed ashore,
There to be fretted by the drag and shove
At the tide's edge, I lie—these things and more:
Whose arm alone between me and the sand,
Whose voice alone, whose pitiful breath brought near,
Could thaw these nostrils and unlock this hand,
She could advise you, should you care to hear.
Small chance, however, in a storm so black,
A man will leave his friendly fire and snug
For a drowned woman's sake, and bring her back
To drip and scatter shells upon the rug.
No one but Night, with tears on her dark face,
Watches beside me in this windy place.

XX

Think not, nor for a moment let your mind,
Wearied with thinking, doze upon the thought
That the work's done and the long day behind,
And beauty, since 'tis paid for, can be bought.
If in the moonlight from the silent bough
Suddenly with precision speak your name
The nightingale, be not assured that now
His wing is limed and his wild virtue tame.
Beauty beyond all feathers that have flown
Is free; you shall not hood her to your wrist,
Nor sting her eyes, nor have her for your own
In any fashion; beauty billed and kissed
Is not your turtle; tread her like a dove—
She loves you not; she never heard of love.

XXX

Love is not all: it is not meat nor drink
Nor slumber nor a roof against the rain;
Nor yet a floating spar to men that sink
And rise and sink and rise and sink again;
Love can not fill the thickened lung with breath,
Nor clean the blood, nor set the fractured bone;
Yet many a man is making friends with death
Even as I speak, for lack of love alone.
It well may be that in a difficult hour,
Pinned down by pain and moaning for release,
Or nagged by want past resolution's power,
I might be driven to sell your love for peace,
Or trade the memory of this night for food.
It well may be. I do not think I would.

from *Mine the Harvest*

"I will put Chaos into fourteen lines"

I will put Chaos into fourteen lines
And keep him there; and let him thence escape
If he be lucky; let him twist, and ape
Flood, fire, and demon—his adroit designs
Will strain to nothing in the strict confines
Of this sweet Order, where, in pious rape,
I hold his essence and amorphous shape,
Till he with Order mingles and combines.
Past are the hours, the years, of our duress,
His arrogance, our awful servitude:
I have him. He is nothing more nor less
Than something simple not yet understood;
I shall not even force him to confess;
Or answer. I will only make him good.

from *Epitaph for the Race of Man*

v

When Man is gone and only gods remain
To stride the world, their mighty bodies hung
With golden shields, and golden curls outflung
Above their childish foreheads; when the plain
Round skull of Man is lifted and again
Abandoned by the ebbing wave, among
The sand and pebbles of the beach,—what tongue
Will tell the marvel of the human brain?
Heavy with music once this windy shell,
Heavy with knowledge of the clustered stars;
The one-time tenant of this draughty hall
Himself, in learned pamphlet, did foretell,
After some aeons of study jarred by wars,
This toothy gourd, this head emptied of all.

WILFRED OWEN

Anthem for Doomed Youth

What passing-bells for these who die as cattle?
    Only the monstrous anger of the guns.
    Only the stuttering rifles' rapid rattle
Can pattern out their hasty orisons.
No mockeries for them; no prayers nor bells,
Nor any voice of mourning save the choirs,—
The shrill, demented choirs of wailing shells;
And bugles calling for them from sad shires.

What candles may be held to speed them all?
    Not in the hands of boys, but in their eyes
Shall shine the holy glimmers of good-byes.
    The pallor of girls' brows shall be their pall;
Their flowers the tenderness of patient minds,
And each slow dusk a drawing-down of blinds.

Dulce et Decorum Est

Bent double, like old beggars under sacks,
Knock-kneed, coughing like hags, we cursed through sludge,
Till on the haunting flares we turned our backs
And towards our distant rest began to trudge.
Men marched asleep. Many had lost their boots
But limped on, blood-shod. All went lame; all blind;
Drunk with fatigue; deaf even to the hoots
Of tired, outstripped Five-Nines that dropped behind.

Gas! GAS! Quick, boys!—An ecstasy of fumbling,
Fitting the clumsy helmets just in time;
But someone still was yelling out and stumbling,
And flound'ring like a man in fire or lime . . .
Dim, through the misty panes and thick green light,
As under a green sea, I saw him drowning.

In all my dreams, before my helpless sight,
He plunges at me, guttering, choking, drowning.

If in smothering dreams you too could pace
Behind the wagon that we flung him in,
And watch the white eyes writhing in his face,
His hanging face, like a devil's sick of sin;
If you could hear, at every jolt, the blood
Come gargling from the froth-corrupted lungs,
Obscene as cancer, bitter as the cud
Of vile, incurable sores on innocent tongues,—
My friend, you would not tell with such high zest
To children ardent for some desperate glory,
The old Lie: Dulce et decorum est
Pro patria mori.

Futility

Move him into the sun—
Gently its touch awoke him once,
At home, whispering of fields half-sown.
Always it woke him, even in France,
Until this morning and this snow.
If anything might rouse him now
The kind old sun will know.

Think how it wakes the seeds—
Woke once the clays of a cold star.
Are limbs, so dear achieved, are sides
Full-nerved, still warm, too hard to stir?
Was it for this, the clay grew tall?
—O what made fatuous sunbeams toil
To break earth's sleep at all?

DOROTHY PARKER

"I Shall Come Back"

I shall come back without fanfaronade
Of wailing wind and graveyard panoply;
But, trembling, slip from cool Eternity—
A mild and most bewildered little shade.
I shall not make sepulchral midnight raid,
But softly come where I had longed to be
In April twilight's unsung melody,
And I, not you, shall be the one afraid.

Strange, that from lovely dreamings of the dead
I shall come back to you, who hurt me most.
You may not feel my hand upon your head,
I'll be so new and inexpert a ghost.
Perhaps you will not know that I am near,—
And that will break my ghostly heart, my dear.

E.E. CUMMINGS

"my girl's tall with hard long eyes"

my girl's tall with hard long eyes
as she stands,with her long hard hands keeping
silence on her dress,good for sleeping
is her long hard body filled with surprise
like a white shocking wire,when she smiles
a hard long smile it sometimes makes
gaily go clean through me tickling aches,
and the weak noise of her eyes easily files
my impatience to an edge—my girl's tall
and taut,with thin legs just like a vine
that's spent all of its life on a garden-wall,
and is going to die.   When we grimly go to bed
with these legs she begins to heave and twine
about me,and to kiss my face and head.

"it may not always be so;and i say"

it may not always be so;and i say
that if your lips,which i have loved,should touch
another's,and your dear strong fingers clutch
his heart,as mine in time not far away;
if on another's face your sweet hair lay
in such a silence as i know,or such
great writhing words as,uttering overmuch,
stand helplessly before the spirit at bay;

if this should be,i say if this should be—
you of my heart,send me a little word;
that i may go unto him,and take his hands,
saying,Accept all happiness from me.
Then shall i turn my face,and hear one bird
sing terribly afar in the lost lands.

"i like my body when it is with your"

i like my body when it is with your
body.   It is so quite new a thing.
Muscles better and nerves more.
i like your body.   i like what it does,
i like its hows.   i like to feel the spine
of your body and its bones,and the trembling
-firm-smooth ness and which i will
again and again and again
kiss,   i like kissing this and that of you,
i like,slowly stroking the,shocking fuzz
of your electric fur,and what-is-it comes
over parting flesh. . . . And eyes big love-crumbs,

and possibly i like the thrill

of under me you so quite new

"next to of course god america i"

"next to of course god america i
love you land of the pilgrims' and so forth oh
say can you see by the dawn's early my
country 'tis of centuries come and go
and are no more what of it we should worry
in every language even deafanddumb
thy sons acclaim your glorious name by gorry
by jingo by gee by gosh by gum
why talk of beauty what could be more beaut-
iful than these heroic happy dead
who rushed like lions to the roaring slaughter
they did not stop to think they died instead
then shall the voice of liberty be mute?"

He spoke. And drank rapidly a glass of water

"if i have made,my lady,intricate"

if i have made,my lady,intricate
imperfect various things chiefly which wrong
your eyes(frailer than most deep dreams are frail)
songs less firm than your body's whitest song
upon my mind—if i have failed to snare
the glance too shy—if through my singing slips
the very skilful strangeness of your smile
the keen primeval silence of your hair

—let the world say "his most wise music stole
nothing from death"—
                              you only will create
(who are so perfectly alive)my shame:
lady through whose profound and fragile lips
the sweet small clumsy feet of April came

into the ragged meadow of my soul.

"i carry your heart with me(i carry it in"

i carry your heart with me(i carry it in
my heart)i am never without it(anywhere
i go you go, my dear;and whatever is done
by only me is your doing,my darling)
                              i fear
no fate(for you are my fate, my sweet)i want
no world(for beautiful you are my world,my true)
and it's you are whatever a moon has always meant
and whatever a sun will always sing is you

here is the deepest secret nobody knows
(here is the root of the root and the bud of the bud
and the sky of the sky of a tree called life;which grows
higher than soul can hope or mind can hide)
and this is the wonder that's keeping the stars apart

i carry your heart(i carry it in my heart)

JEAN TOOMER

November Cotton Flower

Boll-weevil's coming, and the winter's cold,
Made cotton-stalks look rusty, season's old,
And cotton, scarce as any southern snow,
Was vanishing; the branch, so pinched and slow,
Failed in its function as the autumn rake;
Drouth fighting soil had caused the soil to take
All water from the streams; dead birds were found
In wells a hundred feet below the ground—
Such was the season when the flower bloomed.
Old folks were startled, and it soon assumed
Significance. Superstition saw
Something it had never seen before:
Brown eyes that loved without a trace of fear,
Beauty so sudden for that time of year.

ROBERT GRAVES

History of the Word

The Word that in the beginning was the Word
For two or three, but elsewhere spoke unheard,
Found Words to interpret it, which for a season
Prevailed until ruled out by Law and Reason
Which, by a lax interpretation cursed,
In Laws and Reasons logically dispersed;
These, in their turn, found they could do no better
Than fall to Letters and each claim a letter.
In the beginning then, the Word alone,
But now the various tongue-tied Lexicon
In perfect impotence the day nearing
When every ear shall lose its sense of hearing
And every mind by knowledge be close-shuttered—
But two or three, that hear the Word uttered.

EDMUND BLUNDEN

Vlamertinghe: Passing the Chateau, July 1917

"And all her silken flanks with garlands drest"—
But we are coming to the sacrifice.
Must those have flowers who are not yet gone West?
May those have flowers who live with death and lice?
This must be the floweriest place
That earth allows; the queenly face
Of the proud mansion borrows grace for grace
Spite of those brute guns lowing at the skies.

Bold great daisies, golden lights,
Bubbling roses' pinks and whites—
Such a gay carpet! poppies by the million;
Such damask! such vermilion!
But if you ask me, mate, the choice of colour
Is scarcely right; this red should have been much duller.

LOUISE BOGAN

Simple Autumnal

The measured blood beats out the year's delay.
The tearless eyes and heart, forbidden grief,
Watch the burned, restless, but abiding leaf,
The brighter branches arming the bright day.

The cone, the curving fruit should fall away,
The vine stem crumble, ripe grain know its sheaf.
Bonded to time, fires should have done, be brief,
But, serfs to sleep, they glitter and they stay.

Because not last nor first, grief in its prime
Wakes in the day, and hears of life's intent.
Sorrow would break the seal stamped over time
And set the baskets where the bough is bent.

Full season's come, yet filled trees keep the sky
And never scent the ground where they must lie.

Single Sonnet

Now, you great stanza, you heroic mould,
Bend to my will, for I must give you love:
The weight in the heart that breathes, but cannot move,
Which to endure flesh only makes so bold.

Take up, take up, as it were lead or gold
The burden; test the dreadful mass thereof.
No stone, slate, metal under or above
Earth, is so ponderous, so dull, so cold.

Too long as ocean bed bears up the ocean,
As earth's core bears the earth, have I borne this;
Too long have lovers, bending for their kiss,
Felt bitter force cohering without motion.

Staunch meter, great song, it is yours, at length,
To prove how stronger you are than my strength.

Musician

Where have these hands been,
By what delayed,
That so long stayed
Apart from the thin

Strings which they now grace
With their lonely skill?
Music and their cool will
At last interlace.

Now with great ease, and slow,
The thumb, the finger, the strong
Delicate hand plucks the long
String it was born to know.

And, under the palm, the string
Sings as it wished to sing.

HART CRANE

To Emily Dickinson

You who desired so much—in vain to ask—
Yet fed your hunger like an endless task,
Dared dignify the labor, bless the quest—
Achieved that stillness ultimately best,

Being, of all, least sought for: Emily, hear!
O sweet, dead Silencer, most suddenly clear
When singing that Eternity possessed
And plundered momently in every breast;

—Truly no flower yet withers in your hand,
The harvest you descried and understand
Needs more than wit to gather, love to bind.
Some reconcilement of remotest mind—

Leaves Ormus rubyless, and Ophir chill.
Else tears heap all within one clay-cold hill.

ROY CAMPBELL

Luis de Camões

Camões, alone, of all the lyric race,
Born in the angry morning of disaster,
Can look a common soldier in the face:
I find a comrade where I sought a master:
For daily, while the stinking crocodiles
Glide from the mangroves on the swampy shore,
He shares my awning on the dhow, he smiles,
And tells me that he lived it all before.
Through fire and shipwreck, pestilence and loss,
Led by the ignis fatuus of duty
To a dog's death—yet of his sorrows king—
He shouldered high his voluntary Cross,
Wrestled his hardships into forms of beauty,
And taught his gorgon destinies to sing.

COUNTEE CULLEN

Yet Do I Marvel

I doubt not God is good, well-meaning, kind,
And did He stoop to quibble could tell why
The little buried mole continues blind,
Why flesh that mirrors Him must some day die,
Make plain the reason tortured Tantalus
Is baited by the fickle fruit, declare
If merely brute caprice dooms Sisyphus
To struggle up a never-ending stair.
Inscrutable His ways are, and immune
To catechism by a mind too strewn
With petty cares to slightly understand
What awful brain compels His awful hand.
Yet do I marvel at this curious thing:
To make a poet black, and bid him sing!

At the Wailing Wall in Jerusalem

Of all the grandeur that was Solomon's
High testament of Israel's far pride,
Shedding its lustre like a sun of suns,
This feeble flicker only has not died.
This wall alone reminds a vanquished race,
This brief remembrance still retained in stone,
That sure foundations guard their given place
To rehabilitate the overthrown.

So in the battered temple of the heart,
That grief is harder on than time on stone,
Though three sides crumble, one will stand apart,
Where thought may mourn its past, remembrance groan,
And hands now bare that once were rich with rings
Rebuild upon the ancient site of things.

PATRICK KAVANAUGH

Canal Bank Walk

Leafy-with-love banks and the green waters of the canal
Pouring redemption for me, that I do
The will of God, wallow in the habitual, the banal,
Grow with nature again as before I grew.
The bright stick trapped, the breeze adding a third
Party to the couple kissing on an old seat,
And a bird gathering materials for the nest for the Word
Eloquently new and abandoned to its delirious beat.
O unworn world enrapture me, encapture me in a web
Of fabulous grass and eternal voices by a beech,
Feed the gaping need of my senses, give me ad lib
To pray unselfconsciously with overflowing speech
For this soul needs to be honoured with a new dress woven
From green and blue things and arguments that cannot be proven.

W. H. AUDEN

Who's Who

A shilling life will give you all the facts:
How Father beat him, how he ran away,
What were the struggles of his youth, what acts
Made him the greatest figure of his day:
Of how he fought, fished, hunted, worked all night,
Though giddy, climbed new mountains; named a sea:
Some of the last researchers even write
Love made him weep his pints like you and me.

With all his honours on, he sighed for one
Who, say astonished critics, lived at home;
Did little jobs about the house with skill
And nothing else; could whistle; would sit still
Or potter round the garden; answered some
Of his long marvellous letters but kept none.

Our Bias

The hour-glass whispers to the lion's paw,
The clock-towers tell the gardens day and night,
How many errors Time has patience for,
How wrong they are in being always right.

Yet Time, however loud its chimes or deep,
However fast its falling torrent flows,
Has never put the lion off his leap
Nor shaken the assurance of the rose.

For they, it seems, care only for success:
While we choose words according to their sound
And judge a problem by its awkwardness;

And Time with us was always popular.
When have we not preferred some going round
To going straight to where we are?

Brussels in Winter

Wandering the cold streets tangled like old string,
Coming on fountains silent in the frost,
The city still escapes you; it has lost
The qualities that say "I am a Thing."

Only the homeless and the really humbled
Seem to be sure exactly where they are,
And in their misery are all assembled;
The winter holds them like the Opera.

Ridges of rich apartments rise tonight
Where isolated windows glow like farms:
A phrase goes packed with meaning like a van,

A look contains the history of man,
And fifty francs will earn the stranger right
To warm the heartless city in his arms.

from *The Quest: A Sonnet Sequence*

The Door

Out of it steps the future of the poor,
Enigmas, executioners and rules,
Her Majesty in a bad temper or
The red-nosed Fool who makes a fool of fools.

Great persons eye it in the twilight for
A past it might so carelessly let in,
A widow with a missionary grin,
The foaming inundation at a roar.

We pile our all against it when afraid,
And beat upon its panels when we die:
By happening to be open once, it made

Enormous Alice see a wonderland
That waited for her in the sunshine, and,
Simply by being tiny, made her cry.

from *In Time of War*

XII
And the age ended, and the last deliverer died
In bed, grown idle and unhappy; they were safe:
The sudden shadow of the giant's enormous calf
Would fall no more at dusk across the lawn outside.

They slept in peace: in marshes here and there no doubt
A sterile dragon lingered to a natural death,
But in a year the spoor had vanished from the heath;
The kobold's knocking in the mountain petered out.

Only the sculptors and the poets were half sad,
And the pert retinue from the magician's house
Grumbled and went elsewhere. The vanquished powers were glad

To be invisible and free: without remorse
Struck down the sons who strayed into their course,
And ravished the daughters, and drove the fathers mad.

XXVII

Wandering lost upon the mountains of our choice,
Again and again we sigh for an ancient South,
For the warm nude ages of instinctive poise,
For the taste of joy in the innocent mouth.

Asleep in our huts, how we dream of a part
In the glorious balls of the future; each intricate maze
Has a plan, and the disciplined movements of the heart
Can follow for ever and ever its harmless ways.

We envy streams and houses that are sure:
But we are articled to error; we
Were never nude and calm like a great door,

And never will be perfect like the fountains;
We live in freedom by necessity,
A mountain people dwelling among mountains.

LOUIS MacNEICE

Sunday Morning

Down the road someone is practicing scales,
The notes like little fishes vanish with a wink of tails,
Man's heart expands to tinker with his car
For this is Sunday morning, Fate's great bazaar,
Regard these means as ends, concentrate on this Now,
And you may grow to music or drive beyond Hindhead anyhow,
Take corners on two wheels until you go so fast
That you can clutch a fringe or two of the windy past,
That you can abstract this day and make it to the week of time
A small eternity, a sonnet self-contained in rhyme.

But listen, up the road, something gulps, the church spire
Opens its eight bells out, skulls' mouths which will not tire
To tell how there is no music or movement which secures
Escape from the weekday time. Which deadens and endures.

MALCOLM LOWRY

Delirium in Vera Cruz

Where has tenderness gone, he asked the mirror
Of the Biltmore Hotel, cuarto 216. Alas,
Can its reflection lean against the glass
Too, wondering where I have gone, into what horror?
Is that it staring at me now with terror
Behind your frail tilted barrier? Tenderness
Was here, in this very bedroom, in this
Place, its form seen, cries heard, by you. What error
Is here? Am I that rashed image?
Is this the ghost of the love you reflected?
Now with a background of tequila, stubs, dirty collars,
Sodium perborate, and a scrawled page
To the dead, telephone off the hook? In rage
He smashed all the glass in the room. (Bill: $50.)

STEPHEN SPENDER

"Without that once clear aim, the path of flight"

Without that once clear aim, the path of flight
To follow for a lifetime through white air,
This century chokes me under roots of night
I suffer like history in Dark Ages, where
Truth lies in dungeons, from which drifts no whisper:
We hear of towers long broken off from sight
And tortures and war, in dark and smoky rumor,
But on men's buried lives there falls no light.
Watch me who walk through coiling streets where rain
And fog drown every cry: at corners of day
Road drills explore new areas of pain,
Nor summer nor light may reach down here to play.
The city builds its horror in my brain,
This writing is my only wings away.

ELIZABETH BISHOP

The Prodigal

The brown enormous odor he lived by
was too close, with its breathing and thick hair,
for him to judge. The floor was rotten; the sty
was plastered halfway up with glass-smooth dung.
Light-lashed, self-righteous, above moving snouts,
the pigs' eyes followed him, a cheerful stare—
even to the sow that always ate her young—
till, sickening, he leaned to scratch her head.
But sometimes mornings after drinking bouts
(he hid the pints behind a two-by-four),
the sunrise glazed the barnyard mud with red;
the burning puddles seemed to reassure.
And then he thought he almost might endure
his exile yet another year or more.

But evenings the first star came to warn.
The farmer whom he worked for came at dark
to shut the cows and horses in the barn
beneath their overhanging clouds of hay,
with pitchforks, faint forked lightnings, catching light,
safe and companionable as in the Ark.
The pigs stuck out their little feet and snored.
The lantern—like the sun, going away—
laid on the mud a pacing aureole.
Carrying a bucket along a slimy board,
he felt the bats' uncertain staggering flight,
his shuddering insights, beyond his control,
touching him. But it took him a long time
finally to make his mind up to go home.

GEORGE BARKER

To My Mother

Most near, most dear, most loved and most far,
Under the window where I often found her
Sitting as huge as Asia, seismic with laughter,
Gin and chicken helpless in her Irish hand,
Irresistible as Rabelais, but most tender for
The lame dogs and hurt birds that surround her,—
She is a procession no one can follow after
But be like a little dog following a brass band.

She will not glance up at the bomber, or condescend
To drop her gin and scuttle to a cellar,
But leans on the mahogany table like a mountain
Whom only faith can move, and so I send
O all my faith, and all my love to tell her
That she will move from mourning into morning.

ROBERT HAYDEN

Those Winter Sundays

Sundays too my father got up early
and put his clothes on in the blueblack cold,
then with cracked hands that ached
from labor in the weekday weather made
banked fires blaze. No one ever thanked him.

I'd wake and hear the cold splintering, breaking.
When the rooms were warm, he'd call,
and slowly I would rise and dress,
fearing the chronic angers of that house,

Speaking indifferently to him,
who had driven out the cold
and polished my good shoes as well.
What did I know, what did I know
of love's austere and lonely offices.

JOHN BERRYMAN

from *Berryman's Sonnets*

7

I've found out why, that day, that suicide
From the Empire State falling on someone's car
Troubled you so; and why we quarrelled. War,
Illness, an accident, I can see (you cried)
But not this: what a bastard, not spring wide! . .
I said a man, life in his teeth, could care
Not much just whom he spat it on . . and far
Beyond my laugh we argued either side.

"One has a right not to be fallen on! . ."
(Our second meeting . . yellow you were wearing.)
Voices of our resistance and desire!
Did I divine then I must shortly run
Crazy with need to fall on you, despairing?
Did you bolt so, before it caught, our fire?

15

What was Ashore, then? . . Cargoed with Forget,
My ship runs down a midnight winter storm
Between whirlpool and rock, and my white love's form
Gleams at the wheel, her hair streams. When we met
Seaward, Thought frank & guilty to each oar set
Hands careless of port as of the waters' harm.
Endless a wet wind wears my sail, dark swarm
Endless of sighs and veering hopes, love's fret.

Rain of tears, real, mist of imagined scorn,
No rest accords the fraying shrouds, all thwart
Already with mistakes, foresight so short.
Muffled in capes of waves my clear sighs, torn,
Hitherto most clear,—Loyalty and Art.
And I begin now to despair of port.

(after Petrarch and Wyatt)

Keep your eyes open when you kiss: do: when
You kiss. All silly time else, close them to;
Unsleeping, I implore you (dear) pursue
In darkness me, as I do you again
Instantly we part . . only me both then
And when your fingers fall, let there be two
Only, "in that dream-kingdom": I would have you
Me alone recognize your citizen.

Before who wanted eyes, making love, so?
I do now. However we are driven and hide,
What state we keep all other states condemn,
We see ourselves, we watch the solemn glow
Of empty courts we kiss in . . Open wide!
You do, you do, and I look into them.

WELDON KEES

For My Daughter

Looking into my daughter's eyes I read
Beneath the innocence of morning flesh
Concealed, hintings of death she does not heed.
Coldest of winds have blown this hair, and mesh
Of seaweed snarled these miniatures of hands;
The night's slow poison, tolerant and bland,
Has moved her blood. Parched years that I have seen
That may be hers appear: foul, lingering
Death in certain war, the slim legs green.
Or, fed on hate, she relishes the sting
Of others' agony; perhaps the cruel
Bride of a syphilitic or a fool.
These speculations sour in the sun.
I have no daughter. I desire none.

DYLAN THOMAS

Among Those Killed in the Dawn Raid Was a Man Aged a Hundred

When the morning was waking over the war
He put on his clothes and stepped out and he died,
The locks yawned loose and a blast blew them wide,
He dropped where he loved on the burst pavement stone
And the funeral grains of the slaughtered floor.
Tell his street on its back he stopped a sun
And the craters of his eyes grew springshoots and fire
When all the keys shot from the locks, and rang.
Dig no more for the chains of his gray-haired heart.
The heavenly ambulance drawn by a wound
Assembling waits for the spade's ring on the cage.
O keep his bones away from that common cart,
The morning is flying on the wings of his age
And a hundred storks perch on the sun's right hand.

MARGARET WALKER

Childhood

When I was a child I knew red miners
dressed raggedly and wearing carbide lamps.
I saw them come down red hills to their camps
dyed with red dust from old Ishkooda mines.
Night after night I met them on the roads,
or on the streets in town I caught their glance;
the swing of dinner buckets in their hands,
and grumbling undermining all their words.

I also lived in low cotton country
where moonlight hovered over ripe haystacks,
or stumps of trees, and croppers' rotting shacks
with famine, terror, flood, and plague near by;
where sentiment and hatred still held sway
and only bitter land was washed away.

GWENDOLYN BROOKS

from *Gay Chaps at the Bar*

gay chaps at the bar

*. . . and guys I knew in the States, young officers, return from the front
crying and trembling. Gay chaps at the bar in Los Angeles, Chicago,
New York . . .*
                    —LIEUTENANT WILLIAM COUCH IN THE SOUTH PACIFIC

We knew how to order. Just the dash
Necessary. The length of gaiety in good taste.
Whether the raillery should be slightly iced
And given green, or served up hot and lush.
And we knew beautifully how to give to women
The summer spread, the tropics, of our love.
When to persist, or hold a hunger off.
Knew white speech. How to make a look an omen.
But nothing ever taught us to be islands.
And smart, athletic language for this hour
Was not in the curriculum. No stout
Lesson showed how to chat with death. We brought
No brass fortissimo, among our talents,
To holler down the lions in this air.

my dreams, my works, must wait till after hell

I hold my honey and I store my bread
In little jars and cabinets of my will.
I label clearly, and each latch and lid
I bid, Be firm till I return from hell.
I am very hungry. I am incomplete.
And none can tell when I may dine again.
No man can give me any word but Wait,
The puny light. I keep eyes pointed in;
Hoping that, when the devil days of my hurt
Drag out to their last dregs and I resume
On such legs as are left me, in such heart
As I can manage, remember to go home,
My taste will not have turned insensitive
To honey and bread old purity could love.

On a snug evening I shall watch her fingers,
Cleverly ringed, declining to clever pink,
Beg glory from the willing keys. Old hungers
Will break their coffins, rise to eat and thank.
And music, warily, like the golden rose
That sometimes after sunset warms the west,
Will warm that room, persuasively suffuse
That room and me, rejuvenate a past.
But suddenly, across my climbing fever
Of proud delight—a multiplying cry.
A cry of bitter dead men who will never
Attend a gentle maker of musical joy.
Then my thawed eye will go again to ice.
And stone will shove the softness from my face.

from *The Children of the Poor*

I

People who have no children can be hard:
Attain a mail of ice and insolence:
Need not pause in the fire, and in no sense
Hesitate in the hurricane to guard.
And when wide world is bitten and bewarred
They perish purely, waving their spirits hence
Without a trace of grace or of offense
To laugh or fail, diffident, wonder-starred.
While through a throttling dark we others hear
The little lifting helplessness, the queer
Whimper-whine; whose unridiculous
Lost softness softly makes a trap for us.
And makes a curse. And makes a sugar of
The malocclusions, the inconditions of love.

4

First fight. Then fiddle. Ply the slipping string
With feathery sorcery; muzzle the note
With hurting love; the music that they wrote
Bewitch, bewilder. Qualify to sing
Threadwise. Devise no salt, no hempen thing
For the dear instrument to bear. Devote
The bow to silks and honey. Be remote
A while from malice and from murdering.
But first to arms, to armor. Carry hate
In front of you and harmony behind.
Be deaf to music and to beauty blind.
Win war. Rise bloody, maybe not too late
For having first to civilize a space
Wherein to play your violin with grace.

CHARLES CAUSLEY

Autobiography

Now that my seagoing self-possession wavers
I sit and write the letter you will not answer.
The razor at my wrist patiently severs
Passion from thought, of which the flesh is censor.
I walk by the deep canal where moody lovers
Find their Nirvana on each other's tongues,
And in my naked bed the usual fevers
Invade the tropic sense, brambling the lungs.
I am drowned to the sound of seven flooding rivers
The distant Bombay drum and the ghazel dancer,
But the English Sunday, monstrous as India, shivers,
And the voice of the muezzin is the voice of the station announcer.
The wet fields blot the bitterness of the cry,
And I turn from the tactful friend to the candid sky.

ROBERT LOWELL

History

History has to live with what was here,
clutching and close to fumbling all we had—
it is so dull and gruesome how we die,
unlike writing, life never finishes.
Abel was finished; death is not remote,
a flash-in-the-pan electrifies the skeptic,
his cows crowding like skulls against high-voltage wire,
his baby crying all night like a new machine.
As in our Bibles, white-faced, predatory,
the beautiful, mist-drunken hunter's moon ascends—
a child could give it a face: two holes, two holes,
my eyes, my mouth, between them a skull's no-nose—
O there's a terrifying innocence in my face
drenched with the silver salvage of the mornfrost.

Fishnet

Any clear thing that blinds us with surprise,
your wandering silences and bright trouvailles,
dolphin let loose to catch the flashing fish . . .
saying too little, then too much.
Poets die adolescents, their beat embalms them,
the archetypal voices sing offkey;
the old actor cannot read his friends,
and nevertheless he reads himself aloud,
genius hums the auditorium dead.
The line must terminate.
Yet my heart rises, I know I've gladdened a lifetime
knotting, undoing a fishnet of tarred rope;
the net will hang on the wall when the fish are eaten,
nailed like illegible bronze on the futureless future.

Dolphin

My Dolphin, you only guide me by surprise,
captive as Racine, the man of craft,
drawn through his maze of iron composition
by the incomparable wandering voice of Phèdre.
When I was troubled in mind, you made for my body
caught in its hangman's-knot of sinking lines,
the glassy bowing and scraping of my will. . . .
I have sat and listened to too many
words of the collaborating muse,
and plotted perhaps too freely with my life,
not avoiding injury to others,
not avoiding injury to myself—
to ask compassion . . . this book, half fiction,
an eelnet made by man for the eel fighting—

my eyes have seen what my hand did.

WILLIAM MEREDITH

The Illiterate

Touching your goodness, I am like a man
Who turns a letter over in his hand
And you might think this was because the hand
Was unfamiliar but, truth is, the man
Has never had a letter from anyone;
And now he is both afraid of what it means
And ashamed because he has no other means
To find out what it says than to ask someone.

His uncle could have left the farm to him,
Or his parents died before he sent them word,
Or the dark girl changed and want him for beloved.
Afraid and letter-proud, he keeps it with him.
What would you call his feeling for the words
That keep him rich and orphaned and beloved?

AMY CLAMPITT

The Cormorant in its Element

That bony potbellied arrow, wing pumping along
implacably, with a ramrod's rigid adherence,
airborne, to the horizontal, discloses talents
one would never have guessed at. Plummeting

waterward, big black feet splayed for a landing
gear, slim head turning and turning, vermilion-
strapped, this way and that, with a lightning glance
over the shoulder, the cormorant astounding-

ly, in one sleek involuted arabesque, a vertical
turn on a dime, goes into that inimitable
vanishing-and-emerging-from-under-the-briny-

deep act which, unlike the works of Homo Houdini,
is performed for reasons having nothing at all
to do with ego, guilt, ambition, or even money.

HOWARD NEMEROV

A Primer of the Daily Round

A peels an apple, while B kneels to God,
C telephones to D, who has a hand
On E's knee, F coughs, G turns up the sod
For H's grave, I do not understand
But J is bringing one clay pigeon down
While K brings down a nightstick on L's head,
And M takes mustard, N drives into town,
O goes to bed with P, and Q drops dead,
R lies to S, but happens to be heard
By T, who tells U not to fire V
For having to give W the word
That X is now deceiving Y with Z,
    Who happens just now to remember A
    Peeling an apple somewhere far away.

HAYDEN CARRUTH

from *Sonnets*

3
Last night, I don't know if from habit or intent,
when we lay together you left the door ajar,
a small light in which to see how you are
very beautiful. I saw. And so we spent
ourselves in this private light; the hours went
in a kind of wisdom, the night in a love far
inward drawn to the hot center of our
compassion, which was a wonderment
to me.
        But today in a cold snow-light,
so public and glaring, I have seen a wrong,
a brutal human wrong, done in my sight
to you, and the world I have tried to put in song
is more ugly to me now than I can say.
Love, we must keep our own light through the day.

4
While you stood talking at the counter, cutting
leftover meat for a casserole, out came
a cruelty done you—yes, almost the same
as others, but of such evil I think nothing
could enter my mind like this and be shut in
forever, black and awful. No tears of shame
secreted from all humanity's self-blame
will ever leach it or cover it. What in
this world or out of it, Christ, you horrid
cadaver, permitted you to permit this
to happen to her? Silly to think a kiss
or a sonnet or anything might help: that coward
did what he did. Evil is more than love.
It is consciousness, whatever we're conscious of.

5

From our very high window at the Sheraton
in Montreal, amazed I stood a long time
gazing at Cosmopolis outward and down
in all its million glitterings, I who am
a countryman temerarious and lost
like our planet in the great galaxy,
one spark, one speck, one instant, yet the most
part of my thought was not displeasing to me,
but rather an excitement, a dare that could
still raise my pulse-rate after these sixty years
to exult in humanity so variable and odd
and burgeoning, so that bewildered tears
stood briefly in my eyes when we went to bed.
For hours we made love and the night sped.

Late Sonnet

For that the sonnet no doubt was my own true
singing and suchlike other song, for that
I gave it up half-coldheartedly to set
my lines in a fashion that proclaimed its virtue
original in young arrogant artificers who
had not my geniality nor voice, and yet
their fashionableness was persuasive to me,—what
shame and sorrow I pay!
                              And that I knew
that beautiful hot old man Sidney Bechet
and heard his music often but not what he
was saying, that tone, phrasing, and free play
of feeling mean more than originality,
these being the actual qualities of song.
Nor is it essential to be young.

MARIE PONSOT

Call

Child like a candelabra at the head
of my bed, wake in me & watch me as
I sleep; maintain your childlife undistracted
where, at the borders of its light, it has
such dulcet limits it becomes the dark.
Maintain against my hungry selfishness
your simple gaze where fear has left no mark.

Today my dead mother to my distress
said on the dreamphone, "Marie, I'll come read
to you," hung up, & in her usual dress
came & stood here. Cold—though I know I need
her true message—I faced her with tenderness
& said, "This isn't right," & she agreed.

Child, watched by your deeper sleep, I may yet say yes.

RICHARD WILBUR

Praise in Summer

Obscurely yet most surely called to praise,
As sometimes summer calls us all, I said
The hills are heavens full of branching ways
Where star-nosed moles fly overhead the dead;
I said the trees are mines in air, I said
See how the sparrow burrows in the sky!
And then I wondered why this mad *instead*
Perverts our praise to uncreation, why
Such savor's in this wrenching things awry.
Does sense so stale that it must needs derange
The world to know it? To a praiseful eye
Should it not be enough of fresh and strange
That trees grow green, and moles can course in clay,
And sparrows sweep the ceiling of our day?

PHILIP LARKIN

"Love, we must part now: do not let it be"

Love, we must part now: do not let it be
Calamitous and bitter. In the past
There has been too much moonlight and self-pity:
Let us have done with it: for now at last
Never has sun more boldly paced the sky,
Never were hearts more eager to be free,
To kick down worlds, lash forests; you and I
No longer hold them; we are husks, that see
The grain going forward to a different use.

There is regret. Always, there is regret.
But it is better that our lives unloose,
As two tall ships, wind-mastered, wet with light,
Break from an estuary with their courses set,
And waving part, and waving drop from sight.

ANTHONY HECHT

Double Sonnet

I recall everything, but more than all,
Words being nothing now, an ease that ever
Remembers her to my unfailing fever,
How she came forward to me, letting fall
Lamplight upon her dress till every small
Motion made visible seemed no mere endeavor
Of body to articulate its offer,
But more a grace won by the way from all
Striving in what is difficult, from all
Losses, so that she moved but to discover
A practice of the blood, as the gulls hover,
Winged with their life, above the harbor wall,
Tracing inflected silence in the tall
Air with a tilt of mastery and quiver
Against the light, as the light fell to favor
Her coming forth; this chiefly I recall.

It is a part of pride, guiding the hand
At the piano in the splash and passage
Of sacred dolphins, making numbers human
By sheer extravagance that can command
Pythagorean heavens to spell their message
Of some unlooked-for peace, out of the common;
Taking no thought at all that man and woman,
Lost in a trance of lamplight, felt the presage
Of the unbidden terror and bone hand
Of gracelessness, and the unspoken omen
That yet shall render all, by its first usage,
Speechless, inept, and totally unmanned.

JANE COOPER

Praise

But I love this poor earth,
because I have not seen another. . . . —OSIP MANDELSTAM

Between five and fifty
most people construct a little lifetime:
they fall in love, make kids, they suffer
and pitch the usual tents of understanding.
But I have built a few unexpected bridges.
Out of inert stone, with its longing to embrace inert stone,
I have sent a few vaults into stainless air.
Is this enough—when I love our poor sister earth?
Sister earth, I kneel and ask pardon.
A clod of turf is no less than inert stone.
Nothing is enough!
In this field set free for our play
who could have foretold
I would live to write at fifty?

DONALD JUSTICE

The Wall

The walls surrounding them they never saw;
The angels, often. Angels were as common
As birds or butterflies, but looked more human.
As long as the wings were furled, they felt no awe.
Beasts, too, were friendly. They could find no flaw
In all of Eden: this was the first omen.
The second was the dream which woke the woman.
She dreamed she saw the lion sharpen his claw.
As for the fruit, it had no taste at all.
They had been warned of what was bound to happen.
They had been told of something called the world.
They had been told and told about the wall.
They saw it now; the gate was standing open.
As they advanced, the giant wings unfurled.

for John Berryman

JAMES K. BAXTER

from *Jerusalem Sonnets*

(Poems for Colin Durning)

I
The small gray cloudy louse that nests in my beard
Is not, as some have called it, "a pearl of God"—

No, it is a fiery tormentor
Waking me at two a.m.

Or thereabouts, when the lights are still on
In the houses in the pa, to go across thick grass

Wet with rain, feet cold, to kneel
For an hour or two in front of the red flickering

Tabernacle light—what He sees inside
My meandering mind I can only guess—

A madman, a nobody, a raconteur
Whom He can joke with—"Lord," I ask Him,

"Do You or don't You expect me to put up with lice?"
His silent laugh still shakes the hills at dawn.

JAMES MERRILL

Marsyas

I used to write in the café sometimes:
Poems on menus, read all over town
Or talked out before ever written down.
One day a girl brought in his latest book.
I opened it—stiff rhythms, gorgeous rhymes—
And made a face. Then crash! my cup upset.
Of twenty upward looks mine only met
His, that gold archaic lion's look

Wherein I saw my wiry person skinned
Of every skill it labored to acquire
And heard the plucked nerve's elemental twang.
They found me dangling where his golden wind
Inflicted so much music on the lyre
That no one could have told you what he sang.

JOHN ASHBERY

Rain Moving In

The blackboard is erased in the attic
And the wind turns up the light of the stars,
Sinewy now. Someone will find out, someone will know.
And if somewhere on this great planet
The truth is discovered, a patch of it, dried, glazed by the sun,
It will just hang on, in its own infamy, humility. No one
Will be better for it, but things can't get any worse.
Just keep playing, mastering as you do the step
Into disorder this one meant. Don't you see
It's all we can do? Meanwhile, great fires
Arise, as of haystacks aflame. The dial has been set
And that's ominous, but all your graciousness in living
Conspires with it, now that this is our home:
A place to be from, and have people ask about.

W. S. MERWIN

Substance

I could see that there was a kind of distance lighted
    behind the face of that time in its very days
as they appeared to me but I could not think of any
    words that spoke of it truly nor point to anything
except what was there at the moment it was beginning
    to be gone and certainly it could not have been proven
nor held however I might reach toward it touching
    the warm lichens the features of the stones the skin
of the river and I could tell then that it was
    the animals themselves that were the weight and place
of the hour as it happened and that the mass of the cow's neck
    the flash of the swallow the trout's flutter were
where it was coming to pass they were bearing the sense of it
    without questions through the speechless cloud of light

JAMES WRIGHT

Saint Judas

When I went out to kill myself, I caught
A pack of hoodlums beating up a man.
Running to spare his suffering, I forgot
My name, my number, how my day began,
How soldiers milled around the garden stone
And sang amusing songs; how all that day
Their javelins measured crowds; how I alone
Bargained the proper coins, and slipped away.

Banished from heaven, I found this victim beaten,
Stripped, kneed, and left to cry. Dropping my rope
Aside, I ran, ignored the uniforms:
Then I remembered bread my flesh had eaten,
The kiss that ate my flesh. Flayed without hope,
I held the man for nothing in my arms.

DONALD HALL

President and Poet

Granted that what we summon is absurd·
Mustaches and the stick, the New York fake
In cowboy costume grinning for the sake
Of cameras that always just occurred;
Granted that his Rough Riders fought a third-
Rate army badly general'd, to make
Headlines for Mr. Hearst: that one can take
Trust-busting not exactly at its word:

Robinson, alcoholic and unread,
Received a letter with a White House frank.
To court the Muse, you'd think T.R.'d've killed her
And had her stuffed, and yet this mountebank
Chose to belaurel Robinson instead
Of famous men like Richard Watson Gilder.

THOM GUNN

First Meeting with a Possible Mother-in-Law

She thought, without the benefit of knowing,
You, who had been hers, were not any more.
We had locked our love in to leave nothing showing
From the room her handiwork had crammed before;
But—much revealing in its figured sewing—
A piece of stuff hung out, caught in the door.
I caused the same suspicion I watched growing:
Who could not tell what whole the part stood for?

There was small likeness between her and me:
Two strangers left upon a bare top landing,
I for a prudent while, she totally.

But, eyes turned from the bright material hint,
Each shared too long a second's understanding,
Learning the other's terms of banishment.

Keats at Highgate

A cheerful youth joined Coleridge on his walk
("Loose," noted Coleridge, "slack, and not well-dressed")
Listening respectfully to the talk talk talk
Of First and Second Consciousness, then pressed
The famous hand with warmth and sauntered back
Homeward in his own state of less dispersed
More passive consciousness—passive, not slack,
Whether of Secondary type or First.

He made his way toward Hampstead so alert
He hardly passed the small grey ponds below
Or watched a sparrow pecking in the dirt
Without some insight swelling the mind's flow
That banks made swift. Everything put to use.
Perhaps not well-dressed but oh no not loose.

JOHN HOLLANDER

from *Powers of Thirteen*

That other time of day when the chiming of Thirteen
Marks the hour in truth comes after midnight has made
Its unseen appearance. Then the whole trembling house starts
Gathering itself together in sudden fear, creaks
On the stairs grow tacit, and, even outside, the wind
In the lindens has been hushed. Unlike the time beyond
Noon, when your visitations shape that original
Hour, when we pull the shades down in our space between
Moments totally contiguous in the clocked world,
This black gap between days is no place for us: should you
Creep into my bed then you would find me shuddering
As at the opening of a secret whose shadowed
Power unbroken lay in coupling day unto day.

from *The Mad Potter* [closing stanza]

Clay to clay: Soon I shall indeed become
Dumb as these solid cups of hardened mud
(Dull *terra cruda* colored like our blood);
Meanwhile the slap and thump of palm and thumb
On wet mis-shapenness begins to hum
With meaning that was silent for so long.
The words of my wheel's turning come to ring
Truer than Truth itself does, my great *Ding
Dong-an-sich* that echoes everything
(Against it even lovely bells ring wrong):
Its whole voice gathers up the purest parts
Of all our speech, the vowels of the earth,
The aspirations of our hopeful hearts
Or the prophetic sibillance of song.

ADRIENNE RICH

from *Contradictions: Tracking Poems*

18
The problem, unstated till now, is how
to live in a damaged body
in a world where pain is meant to be gagged
uncured   un-grieved over   The problem is
to connect, without hysteria, the pain
of any one's body with the pain of the body's world
For it is the body's world
they are trying to destroy forever
The best world is the body's world
filled with creatures   filled with dread
misshapen so   yet the best we have
our raft among the abstract worlds
and how I longed to live on this earth
walking her boundaries   never counting the cost

it will not be simple, it will not be long
it will take little time, it will take all your thought
it will take all your heart, it will take all your breath
it will be short, it will not be simple

it will touch through your ribs, it will take all your heart
it will not be long, it will occupy your thought
as a city is occupied, as a bed is occupied
it will take all your flesh, it will not be simple

You are coming into us who cannot withstand you
you are coming into us who never wanted to withstand you
you are taking parts of us into places never planned
you are going far away with pieces of our lives

it will be short, it will take all your breath
it will not be simple, it will become your will

DEREK WALCOTT

Homage to Edward Thomas

Formal, informal, by a country's cast
topography delineates its verse,
erects the classic bulk, for rigid contrast
of sonnet, rectory or this manor house
dourly timbered against these sinuous
Downs, defines the formal and informal prose
of Edward Thomas's poems, which make this garden
return its subtle scent of Edward Thomas
in everything here hedged or loosely grown.
Lines which you once dismissed as tenuous
because they would not howl or overwhelm,
as crookedly grave-bent, or cuckoo-dreaming,
seeming dissoluble as this Sussex down
harden in their indifference, like this elm.

GEOFFREY HILL

September Song
born 19.6.32—deported 24.9.42

Undesirable you may have been, untouchable
you were not. Not forgotten
or passed over at the proper time.

As estimated, you died. Things marched,
sufficient, to that end.
Just so much Zyklon and leather, patented
terror, so many routine cries.

(I have made
an elegy for myself it
is true)

September fattens on vines. Roses
flake from the wall. The smoke
of harmless fires drifts to my eyes.

This is plenty. This is more than enough.

SYLVIA PLATH

Mayflower

Throughout black winter the red haws withstood
Assault of snow-flawed winds from the dour skies
And, bright as blood-drops, proved no brave branch dies
If root's firm-fixed and resolution good.
Now, as green sap ascends the steepled wood,
Each hedge with such white bloom astounds our eyes
As sprang from Joseph's rod, and testifies
How best beauty's born of hardihood.

So when staunch island stock chose forfeiture
Of the homeland hearth to plough their pilgrim way
Across Atlantic furrows, dark, unsure—
Remembering the white, triumphant spray
On hawthorn boughs, with goodwill to endure
They named their ship after the flower of May.

JOHN UPDIKE

Island Cities

You see them from airplanes, nameless green islands
in the oceanic, rectilinear plains,
twenty or thirty blocks, compact, but with
everything needed visibly in place—
the high-school playing fields, the swatch of park
along the crooked river, the feeder highways,
the main drag like a zipper, outlying malls
sliced from dirt-colored cakes of plowed farmland.

Small lives, we think—pat, flat—in such tight grids.
But, much like brains with every crease CAT-scanned,
these cities keep their secrets: vagaries
of the spirit, groundwater that floods
the nearby quarries and turns them skyey blue,
dewdrops of longing, jewels, boxed in these blocks.

JEAN VALENTINE

Rain

Snakes of water and light in the window
snakes that shrug out of their skins and follow
pushing a path with their heads full of light
—heavy trembling mercury headlights—
leaving trails of clear grass, and rocks,
nests where they half live, half sleep,
above ground:
Snake where do you come from?
who leave your grass path
and follow me wordless
into our glass
water and light house,
earth wet on your mouth,
you the ground of my underground.

ROBERT MEZEY

Hardy

Thrown away at birth, he was recovered,
Plucked from the swaddling-shroud, and chafed and slapped,
The crone implacable. At last he shivered,
Drew the first breath, and howled, and lay there, trapped
In a world from which there is but one escape
And that forestalled now almost ninety years.
In such a scene as he himself might shape,
The maker of a thousand songs appears.

From this it follows, all the ironies
Life plays on one whose fate it is to follow
The way of things, the suffering one sees,
The many cups of bitterness he must swallow
Before he is permitted to be gone
Where he was headed in that early dawn.

GRACE SCHULMAN

The Abbess of Whitby

There must have been an angel at his ear
When Caedmon gathered up his praise and sang,
Trembling in a barn, of the beginning,
Startled at words he never knew were there.

I heard a voice strike thunder in the air:
Of many kings, only one god is king!
There must have been an angel at his ear
When Caedmon gathered up his praise and sang.

When Caedmon turned in fear from songs of war,
Gleemen who sang the glories of the king
And holy men wondered that so great a power
Could whirl in darkness and force up his song;
There must have been an angel at his ear
When Caedmon gathered up his praise and sang.

CHARLES WRIGHT

Composition in Grey and Pink

The souls of the day's dead fly up like birds, big sister,
The sky shutters and casts loose.
And faster than stars the body goes to the earth.

Heat hangs like a mist from the trees.
Butterflies pump through the banked fires of late afternoon.
The rose continues its sure rise to the self.

Ashes, trampled garlands . . .

I dream of an incandescent space
                              where nothing distinct exists,
And where nothing ends, the days sliding like warm milk through
        the clouds,
Everyone's name in chalk letters once and for all,

The dogstar descending with its pestilent breath . . .

Fatherless, stiller than still water,
I want to complete my flesh
                              and sit in a quiet corner
Untied from God, where the dead don't sing in their sleep.

JUNE JORDAN

Sunflower Sonnet Number Two

Supposing we could just go on and on as two
voracious in the days apart as well as when
we side by side (the many ways we do
that) well! I would consider then
perfection possible, or else worthwhile
to think about. Which is to say
I guess the costs of long term tend to pile
up, block and complicate, erase away
the accidental, temporary, near
thing/pulsebeat promises one makes
because the chance, the easy new, is there
in front of you. But still, perfection takes
some sacrifice of falling stars for rare.
And there are stars, but none of you, to spare.

JUDITH RODRIGUEZ

In-flight Note

Kitten, writes the mousy boy in his neat
fawn casuals sitting beside me on the flight,
neatly, *I can't give up everything just like that.*
Everything, how much was it, and just like what?
Did she cool it or walk out? Loosen her hand from his tight
white-knuckled hand, or not meet him, just as he thought
*You mean far too much to me. I can't forget
the four months we've known each other.* No, he won't eat,
finally he pays—pale, careful, distraught—
for a beer, turns over the page he wrote
and sleeps a bit. Or dreams of his Sydney cat.
The pad cost one dollar twenty. He wakes to write
It's naïve to think we could just be good friends.
Pages and pages. And so the whole world ends.

FREDERICK SEIDEL

Elms

It sang without a sound: music that
The naive elm trees loved. They were alive.
Oh silky music no elm tree could survive.
The head low slither of a stalking cat,
Black panther darkness pouring to the kill,
Entered every elm—they drank it in.
Drank silence. Then the silence drank. Wet chin,
Hot, whiskered darkness. Every elm was ill.
What else is there to give but joy? Disease.
And trauma. Lightning, or as slow as lava.
Darkness drinking from a pool in Java,
Black panther drinking from a dream. The trees
Around the edge are elms. Below, above,
Man-eater drinking its reflection: love.

JOHN FULLER

from Lily and Violin

6
Afterwards we may not speak: piled chords
Are broken open with changes of key;
Logs in settling shoot a surprising flame;
A petal folds more slowly than night falls;
A face is lifted to catch the last
Ache of struggling body or air.

Afterwards we may not speak, since
Everything hastens towards its end
With an enlarging beauty. May not,
Need not, will not, we say, obsessed
Like vagrant creatures with consummation.
But it is all our dear illusion
Belonging to the experience itself
Which must not speak of afterwards.

TONY HARRISON

from *from The School of Eloquence*

On Not Being Milton

> *for Sergio Vieira & Armando Guebuza (Frelimo)*

Read and committed to the flames, I call
these sixteen lines that go back to my roots
my *Cahier d'un retour au pays natal,*
my growing black enough to fit my boots.

The stutter of the scold out of the branks
of condescension, class and counter-class
thickens with glottals to a lumpen mass
of Ludding morphemes closing up their ranks.
Each swung cast-iron Enoch of Leeds stress
clangs a forged music on the frames of Art,
the looms of owned language smashed apart!

Three cheers for mute ingloriousness!

Articulation is the tongue-tied's fighting.
In the silence round all poetry we quote
Tidd the Cato Street conspirator who wrote:

Sir, I Ham a very Bad Hand at Righting.

LES MURRAY

Comete

Uphill in Melbourne on a beautiful day
a woman was walking ahead of her hair.
Like teak oiled soft to fracture and sway
it hung to her heels and seconded her
as a pencilled retinue, an unscrolling title
to ploughland, edged with ripe rows of dress,
a sheathed wing that couldn't fly her at all,
only itself, loosely, and her spirits.
                                        A largesse
of life and self, brushed all calm and out,
its abstracted attempts on her mouth weren't seen,
nor its showering, its tenting. Just the detail
that swam in its flow-lines, glossing about—
as she paced on, comet-like, face to the sun.

CHARLES SIMIC

History

On a gray evening
Of a gray century,
I ate an apple
While no one was looking.

A small, sour apple
The color of woodfire,
Which I first wiped
On my sleeve.

Then I stretched my legs
As far as they'd go,
Said to myself
Why not close my eyes now

Before the Late
World News and Weather.

FRANK BIDART

Self-Portrait, 1969

He's *still* young—; thirty, but looks younger—
or does he? . . . In the eyes and cheeks, tonight,
turning in the mirror, he saw his mother,—
puffy; angry; bewildered . . . Many nights
now, when he stares there, he gets angry:—
something *unfulfilled* there, something dead
to what he once thought he surely could be—
Now, just the glamour of habits . . .

                        Once, instead,
he thought insight would remake him, he'd reach
—what? The thrill, the exhilaration
unravelling disaster, that seemed to teach
necessary knowledge . . . became just jargon.

Sick of being decent, he craves another
crash. What *reaches* him except disaster?

SEAMUS HEANEY

The Forge

All I know is a door into the dark.
Outside, old axles and iron hoops rusting;
Inside, the hammered anvil's short-pitched ring,
The unpredictable fantail of sparks
Or hiss when a new shoe toughens in water.
The anvil must be somewhere in the centre,
Horned as a unicorn, at one end square,
Set there immoveable: an altar
Where he expends himself in shape and music.
Sometimes, leather-aproned, hairs in his nose,
He leans out on the jamb, recalls a clatter
Of hoofs where traffic is flashing in rows;
Then grunts and goes in, with a slam and flick
To beat real iron out, to work the bellows.

Act of Union

I

Tonight, a first movement, a pulse,
As if the rain in bogland gathered head
To slip and flood: a bog-burst,
A gash breaking open the ferny bed.
Your back is a firm line of eastern coast
And arms and legs are thrown
Beyond your gradual hills. I caress
The heaving province where our past has grown.
I am the tall kingdom over your shoulder
That you would neither cajole nor ignore.
Conquest is a lie. I grow older
Conceding your half-independent shore
Within whose borders now my legacy
Culminates inexorably.

II

And I am still imperially
Male, leaving you with the pain,
The rending process in the colony,
The battering ram, the boom burst from within.
The act sprouted an obstinate fifth column
Whose stance is growing unilateral.
His heart beneath your heart is a wardrum
Mustering force. His parasitical
And ignorant little fists already
Beat at your borders and I know they're cocked
At me across the water. No treaty
I foresee will salve completely your tracked
And stretchmarked body, the big pain
That leaves you raw, like opened ground, again.

The Seed Cutters

They seem hundreds of years away. Brueghel,
You'll know them if I can get them true.
They kneel under the hedge in a half-circle
Behind a windbreak wind is breaking through.
They are the seed cutters. The tuck and frill
Of leaf-sprout is on the seed potatoes
Buried under that straw. With time to kill,
They are taking their time. Each sharp knife goes
Lazily halving each root that falls apart
In the palm of the hand: a milky gleam,
And, at the centre, a dark watermark.
Oh, calendar customs! Under the broom
Yellowing over them, compose the frieze
With all of us there, our anonymities.

A Dream of Jealousy

Walking with you and another lady
In wooded parkland, the whispering grass
Ran its fingers through our guessing silence
And the trees opened into a shady
Unexpected clearing where we sat down.
I think the candour of the light dismayed us.
We talked about desire and being jealous,
Our conversation a loose single gown
Or a white picnic tablecloth spread out
Like a book of manners in the wilderness.
"Show me," I said to our companion, "what
I have much coveted, your breast's mauve star."
And she consented. Oh neither these verses
Nor my prudence, love, can heal your wounded stare.

from *Clearances*

II

Polished linoleum shone there. Brass taps shone.
The china cups were very white and big—
An unchipped set with sugar bowl and jug.
The kettle whistled. Sandwich and tea scone
Were present and correct. In case it run,
The butter must be kept out of the sun.
And don't be dropping crumbs. Don't tilt your chair.
Don't reach. Don't point. Don't make noise when you stir.

It is Number 5, New Row, Land of the Dead,
Where grandfather is rising from his place
With spectacles pushed back on a clean bald head
To welcome a bewildered homing daughter
Before she even knocks. "What's this? What's this?"
And they sit down in the shining room together.

III

When all the others were away at Mass
I was all hers as we peeled potatoes.
They broke the silence, let fall one by one
Like solder weeping off the soldering iron:
Cold comforts set between us, things to share
Gleaming in a bucket of clean water.
And again let fall. Little pleasant splashes
From each other's work would bring us to our senses.

So while the parish priest at her bedside
Went hammer and tongs at the prayers for the dying
And some were responding and some crying
I remembered her head bent towards my head,
Her breath in mine, our fluent dipping knives—
Never closer the whole rest of our lives.

STANLEY PLUMLY

from *Boy on the Step*

5
None of us dies entirely—some of us, all
of us sometimes come back sapling, seedling, cell,
like second growth, slowly, imperceptibly,
in the imprint of rings that wind like music
written down, in notes and bars, scale and silence.
Even the child, who was immortal, becomes
purity, anonymity inside us.
Which is why to watch a tree turn into fire
or fall is like a second death, like the grace
in stillness gone, exploded, fatal, final,
as someone loved, within whose face we confused
the infinite with the intimate, is last
a name, the point of a green leaf drawn across
the heart, whose loss is felt, though invisible.

BILLY COLLINS

American Sonnet

We do not speak like Petrarch or wear a hat like Spenser
and it is not fourteen lines
like furrows in a small, carefully plowed field

but the picture postcard, a poem on vacation,
that forces us to sing our songs in little rooms
or pour our sentiments into measuring cups.

We write on the back of a waterfall or lake,
adding to the view a caption as conventional
as an Elizabethan woman's heliocentric eyes.

We locate an adjective for the weather.
We announce that we are having a wonderful time.
We express the wish that you were here

and hide the wish that we were where you are,
walking back from the mailbox, your head lowered
as you read and turn the thin message in your hands.

A slice of this place, a length of white beach,
a piazza or carved spires of a cathedral
will pierce the familiar place where you remain,

and you will toss on the table this reversible display:
a few square inches of where we have strayed
and a compression of what we feel.

Sonnet

All we need is fourteen lines, well, thirteen now,
and after this next one just a dozen
to launch a little ship on love's storm-tossed seas,
then only ten more left like rows of beans.
How easily it goes unless you get Elizabethan
and insist the iambic bongos must be played
and rhymes positioned at the ends of lines,
one for every station of the cross.
But hang on here while we make the turn
into the final six where all will be resolved,
where longing and heartache will find an end,
where Laura will tell Petrarch to put down his pen,
take off those crazy medieval tights,
blow out the lights, and come at last to bed.

DOUGLAS DUNN

France

A dozen sparrows scuttled on the frost.
We watched them play. We stood at the window,
And, if you saw us, then you saw a ghost
In duplicate. I tied her nightgown's bow.
She watched and recognized the passers-by.
Had they looked up, they'd know that she was ill—
"Please, do not draw the curtains when I die"—
From all the flowers on the windowsill.

"It's such a shame," she said. "Too ill, too quick."
"I would have liked us to have gone away."
We closed our eyes together, dreaming France,
Its meadows, rivers, woods and *jouissance*.
I counted summers, our love's arithmetic.
"Some other day, my love. Some other day."

MARILYN HACKER

Sonnet

Love drives its rackety blue caravan
right to the edge. The valley lies below,
unseasonable leaves shading the so-
seemly houses from the sun. We can
climb down. Cornflowers push from crevices
and little purple star-blooms with no name
we know. Look up. I didn't think we came
this far. Look down. No, don't. I think there is
a path between those rocks. Steady. Don't hold
my sleeve, you'll trip me. Oh, Jesus, I've turned
my ankle. Let me just sit down. . . .
Predictably, it's dark. No lights go on
below. There is a dull red glow of burn-
ing at the edge. Predictably, it's cold.

from *Love, Death, and the Changing of the Seasons*

Did you love well what very soon you left?
Come home and take me in your arms and take
away this stomach ache, headache, heartache.
Never so full, I never was bereft
so utterly. The winter evenings drift
dark to the window. Not one word will make
you, where you are, turn in your day, or wake
from your night toward me. The only gift
I got to keep or give is what I've cried,
floodgates let down to mourning for the dead
chances, for the end of being young,
for everyone I loved who really died.
I drank our one year out in brine instead
of honey from the seasons of your tongue.

DAVID HUDDLE

from *Tour of Duty*

Words

What did those girls say when you walked the strip
of tin-shack bars, gewgaw stores, barber shops,
laundries, and restaurants, most all of which
had beds in back, those girls who had to get up
in Saigon before dawn to catch their rides to Cu Chi,
packed ten to a Lambretta, chattering, happy
in their own lovely tongue, on the dusty
circus road to work, but then what did they say?

Come here, talk to me, you handsome, GI,
I miss you, I love you too much, you want
short time, go in back, I don't care, I want
your baby, sorry about that, GI,
you number ten. A history away
I translate dumbly what those girls would say.

CHARLES MARTIN

Easter Sunday, 1985

To take steps toward the reappearance alive of the disappeared is a
subversive act, and measures will be adopted to deal with it.
   —GENERAL OSCAR MEJIA VICTORES, PRESIDENT OF GUATEMALA

In the Palace of the President this morning,
The General is gripped by the suspicion
That those who were disappeared will be returning
In a subversive act of resurrection.

Why do you worry? The disappeared can never
Be brought back from wherever they were taken;
The age of miracles is gone forever;
These are not sleeping, nor will they awaken.

And if some tell you Christ once reappeared
Alive, one Easter morning, that he was seen—
Give them the lie, for who today can find him?

He is perhaps with those who were disappeared,
Broken and killed, flung into some ravine
With his arms safely wired up behind him.

WILLIAM MATTHEWS

Vermin

"What do you want to be when you grow up?"
What child cries out, "An exterminator!"?
One diligent student in Mrs. Taylor's
class will get an ant farm for Christmas, but
he'll not see industry; he'll see dither.
"The ant sets an example for us all,"
wrote Max Beerbohm, a master of dawdle,
"but it is not a good one." These children
don't hope to outlast the doldrums of school
only to heft great weights and work in squads
and die for their queen. Well neither did we.
And we knew what we didn't want to be:
the ones we looked down on, the lambs of God,
blander than snow and slow to be cruel.

LOUISE GLÜCK

Snowdrops

Do you know what I was, how I lived? You know
what despair is; then
winter should have meaning for you.

I did not expect to survive,
earth suppressing me. I didn't expect
to waken again, to feel
in damp earth my body
able to respond again, remembering
after so long how to open again
in the cold light
of earliest spring—

afraid, yes, but among you again
crying yes risk joy

in the raw wind of the new world.

ELLEN BRYANT VOIGT

from *Kyrie*

"Dear Mattie, You're sweet to write me every day"

Dear Mattie, You're sweet to write me every day.
The train was not so bad, I found a seat,
watched the landscape flatten until dark,
ate the lunch you packed, your good chess pie.
I've made a friend, a Carolina man
who looks like Emmett Cocke, same big grin,
square teeth. Curses hard but he can shoot.
Sergeant calls him Pug I don't know why.
It's hot here but we're not here for long.
Most all we do is march and shine our boots.
In the drills they keep us 20 feet apart
on account of sickness in the camp.
In case you think to send more pie, send two.
I'll try to bring you back some French perfume.

"Once the world had had its fill of war"

Once the world had had its fill of war,
in a secret wood, as the countryside lay stunned,
at the hour of the wolf and the vole, in a railroad car,
the generals met and put their weapons down.
Like spring it was, as word passed over all
the pocked and riven ground, and underground;
now the nations sat in a gilded hall,
dividing what they'd keep of what they'd won.

And so the armies could be done with war,
and soldiers trickled home to study peace.
But the old gardens grew a tough new weed,
and the old lives didn't fit as they had before,
and where there'd been the dream, a stranger's face,
and where there'd been the war, an empty sleeve.

EAVAN BOLAND

Yeats in Civil War

In middle age you exchanged the sandals
Of a pilgrim for a Norman keep
in Galway. Civil war started. Vandals
Sacked your country, made off with your sleep.

Somehow you arranged your escape
Aboard a spirit ship which every day
Hoisted sail out of fire and rape.
On that ship your mind was stowaway.

The sun mounted on a wasted place.
But the wind at every door and turn
Blew the smell of honey in your face
Where there was none.
                        Whatever I may learn
You are its sum, struggling to survive—
A fantasy of honey your reprieve.

The Singers

for M.R.

The women who were singers in the West
lived on an unforgiving coast.
I want to ask was there ever one
moment when all of it relented,
when rain and ocean and their own
sense of home were revealed to them
as one and the same?
                    After which
every day was still shaped by weather,
but every night their mouths filled with
Atlantic storms and clouded-over stars
and exhausted birds.
                   And only when the danger
was plain in the music could you know
their true measure of rejoicing in

finding a voice where they found a vision.

Heroic

Sex and history. And skin and bone.
And the oppression of Sunday afternoon.
Bells called the faithful to devotion.

I was still at school and on my own.
And walked and walked and sheltered from the rain.

The patriot was made of drenched stone.
His lips were still speaking. The gun
he held had just killed someone.

I looked up. And looked at him again.
He stared past me without recognition.

I moved my lips and wondered how the rain
would taste if my tongue were made of stone.
And wished it was. And whispered so that no one
could hear it but him: *make me a heroine.*

J. D. McCLATCHY

My Mammogram

I

In the shower, at the shaving mirror or beach,
For years I'd led . . . the unexamined life?
When all along and so easily within reach
(Closer even than the nonexistent wife)

Lay the trouble—naturally enough
Lurking in a useless, overlooked
Mass of fat and old newspaper stuff
About matters I regularly mistook

As a horror story for the opposite sex,
Nothing to do with what at my downtown gym
Are furtively ogled as The Guy's Pecs.

But one side is swollen, the too tender skin
Discolored. So the doctor orders an X-
Ray, and nervously frowns at my nervous grin.

II

Mammography's on the basement floor.
The nurse has an executioner's gentle eyes.
I start to unbutton my shirt. She shuts the door.
Fifty, male, already embarrassed by the size

Of my "breasts," I'm told to put the left one
Up on a smudged, cold, Plexiglas shelf,
Part of a robot half menacing, half glum,
Like a three-dimensional model of the Freudian self.

Angles are calculated. The computer beeps.
Saucers close on a flatness further compressed.
There's an ache near the heart neither dull nor sharp.

The room gets lethal. Casually the nurse retreats
Behind her shield. Anxiety as blithely suggests
I joke about a snapshot for my Christmas card.

III

"No sign of cancer," the radiologist swans
In to say—with just a hint in his tone
That he's done me a personal favor—whereupon
His look darkens. "But what these pictures show . . .

Here, look, you'll notice the gland on the left's
Enlarged. See?" I see an aerial shot
Of Iraq, and nod. "We'll need further tests,
Of course, but I'd bet that what *you've* got

Is a liver problem. Trouble with your estrogen
Levels. It's time, my friend, to take stock.
It happens more often than you'd think to men."

Reeling from its millionth scotch on the rocks,
In other words, my liver's sensed the end.
Why does it come as something less than a shock?

IV

The end of life as I've known it, that is to say—
Testosterone sported like a power tie,
The matching set of drives and dreads that may
Now soon be plumped to whatever new designs

My apparently resentful, androgynous
Inner life has on me. Blind seer?
The Bearded Lady in some provincial circus?
Something that others both desire and fear.

Still, doesn't everyone *long* to be changed,
Transformed to, no matter, a higher or lower state,
To know the leathery D-Day hero's strange

Detachment, the queen bee's dreamy loll?
Yes, but the future each of us blankly awaits
Was long ago written on the genetic wall.

v

So suppose the breasts fill out until I look
Like my own mother . . . ready to nurse a son,
A version of myself, the infant understood
In the end as the way my own death had come.

Or will I in a decade be back here again,
The diagnosis this time not freakish but fatal?
The changes in one's later years all tend,
Until the last one, toward the farcical,

Each of us slowly turned into something that hurts,
Someone we no longer recognize.
If soul is the final shape I shall assume,

(—*A knock at the door. Time to button my shirt*
And head back out into the waiting room.)
Which of my bodies will have been the best disguise?

LEON STOKESBURY

To His Book

Wafer; thin and hard and bitter pill I
    Take from time to time; pillow I have lain
        Too long on; holding the brief dreams, the styled
Dreams, the nightmares, shadows, red flames high
    High up on mountains; wilted zinnias, rain
        On dust, and great weight, the dead dog, and wild
Onions; mastodonic woman who knows how,—
    I'm tired of you, tired of your insane
        Acid eating in the brain. Sharp stones, piled
Particularly, I let you go. Sink, or float, or fly now,
                Bad child.

STAR BLACK

Personals

Approximate and unfulfilled, a devilish nymph
in the underworld seeks huge black swan for fiery
twills in cranium's caverns, gray-matter indifference
preferred, although will take sensitivity, as well,

if inexperience in hell is available, for long-term
committed one-flight stand with ensuing consequences
such as bestial transformations and showering soot.
Nymph will attempt to run, as required, from

dark thwunking destiny. Nymph will not be easy
to acquire, though promised to succumb to aerial fury.
Various disguises necessary, drop chute appreciated.

Do not send photograph, please; visuals confusing,
element of surprise essential, fact of advertisement
accidental. Pretend you don't read and never will.

MARILYN NELSON

Balance

He watch her like a coonhound watch a tree.
What might explain the metamorphosis
he underwent when she paraded by
with tea-cakes, in her fresh and shabby dress?
(As one would carry water from a well—
straight-backed, high-headed, like a diadem,
with careful grace so that no drop will spill—
she balanced, almost brimming, her one name.)

She thinks she something, stuck-up island bitch.
Chopping wood, hanging laundry on the line,
and tantalizingly within his reach,
she honed his body's yearning to a keen,
sharp point. And on that point she balanced life.
That hoe Diverne think she Marse Tyler's wife.

BRUCE SMITH

from In My Father's House

O My Invisible Estate

—Vaughan

Where the afternoon sun blears the city.
Where the high-numbered streets zero
their dignity, we live without irony.
No house but a shadow
of a house, but when we need a shadow
this shadow is ours. The shadow
of a man and his two arms, tenderness
and some hunger that I was rocked in.
And whatever house has been in me since then,
a flesh made and unmade since then,
I find that every churchyard has a stone
that bears our name, Father. Imagine
the monuments to a name so common,
imagine that dark land is what we own.

MOLLY PEACOCK

The Lull

The possum lay on the tracks fully dead.
I'm the kind of person who stops to look.
It was big and white with flies on its head,
a thick healthy hairless tail, and strong, hooked
nails on its racoon-like feet. It was a full-
grown possum. It was sturdy and adult.
Only its head was smashed. In the lull
that it took to look, you took the time to insult
the corpse, the flies, the world, the fact that we were
traipsing in our dress shoes down the railroad tracks.
"That's disgusting." You said that. Dreams, brains, fur
and guts: what we are. That's my bargain, the Pax
Peacock, with the world. Look hard, life's soft. Life's cache
is flesh, flesh, and flesh.

Desire

It doesn't speak and it isn't schooled,
like a small foetal animal with wettened fur.
It is the blind instinct for life unruled,
visceral frankincense and animal myrrh.
It is what babies bring to kings,
an eyes-shut, ears-shut medicine of the heart
that smells and touches endings and beginnings
without the details of time's experienced *part-
fit-into-part-fit-into-part*. Like a paw,
it is blunt; like a pet who knows you
and nudges your knee with its snout—but more raw
and blinder and younger and more divine, too,
than the tamed world—it's the drive for what is real,
deeper than the brain's detail: the drive to feel.

Instead of Her Own

Instead of her own, my grandmother washed my hair.
The porcelain was cold at the back of my neck,
my fragile neck. Altogether it was cold there.

She did it so my hair would smell sweet.
What else is like the moist mouse straw
of a girl's head? Why, the feeling of complete

peace the smell brings to a room whose window
off oily Lake Erie is rimmed with snow.
Knuckles rasping at young temples know,

in the involuntary way a body knows,
that as old is, so young grows. Completion
drives us: substitution is our mission.

Thin little head below thin little head grown old.
Water almost warm in a room almost cold.

HUGH SEIDMAN

14 First Sentences

He had never kept a journal.
Sometimes he wanted to write prose about first love.
Once he heard Auden lecture: Don't falsify history.
He used to feel better if people in novels were rich.
Williams wrote: Old woman, all this was for you.
He was going to type: The form of a life changes little.
Reich said the Eskimos say: Don't thwart a child.
Zukofsky taught: The poet makes one long poem.
Mathematicians say: Notation is notion.
The dream voice said: Imagination fails the dream.
He read in the paper: The poor, mired in poverty.
Sometimes he remembered the books forgotten in libraries.
Do we sleep only because night falls?
How shall one speak how another suffers?

RACHEL HADAS

Moments of Summer

i
Let gleaming motes of hayseed in the barn
be asterisks embedded in the text
of ever after. Over by the lawn
let the hammock be an ampersand
skewed to the horizontal, loosely slung
between an evergreen and larch whose sap
sometimes bedews the dreamer in suspension.
Let the book left open on her lap
and on whose margins scattered symbols mark
tempo as slow, as slower, as quite still,
guide her between this twilight and the next.
The swinging stops. Behind the pine-treed hill
Venus appears to herald in the green
slumber of gardens growing in the dark.

ii
June's supple weavings covered up the dry
tank winter had just drained. So did it fill?
Not yet. The least green gesture halted me.
A sundial blandly bedded among flowers
foreshadows a beginning or an end,
silently tells the passing of the hours:
that promise, that futility, that beauty.
Each summer points to picnics on the hill.
What if what falters is the sheer desire
to scale even our modest little mound,
look over treetops, steeples, see the whole?
Somewhere invisible a chainsaw roars.
Precisely where pines creak and sway and fall
is muffled in imagination's veil.

iii
The horizontal tugs me more and more.
Childhood hours spent reading with my father
rise in a kind procession once again.
Disparate gravities of our two ages
dissolve as we lie back and let the pages
take us, float us, sail us out to sea.
What special spell (not always narrative;
the winter we read "De Senectute"
I was fifteen; you had two years to live)
braided our endless differences to one?
Today a mother reading to my son,
I savor freshly that sweet nourishment,
timeless hours reading motionless together,
especially if we are lying down.

DENIS JOHNSON

Sway

Since I find you will no longer love,
from bar to bar in terror I shall move
past Forty-third and Halsted, Twenty-fourth
and Roosevelt where fire-gutted cars,
their bones the bones of coyote and hyena,
suffer the light from the wrestling arena
to fall all over them. And what they say
blends in the tarantellasmic sway
of all of us between the two of these:
harmony and divergence,
their sad story of harmony and divergence,
the story that begins
I did not know who she was
and ends *I did not know who she was.*

Passengers

The world will burst like an intestine in the sun,
the dark turn to granite and the granite to a name,
but there will always be somebody riding the bus
through these intersections strewn with broken glass
among speechless women beating their little ones,
always a slow alphabet of rain
speaking of drifting and perishing to the air,
always these definite jails of light in the sky
at the wedding of this clarity and this storm
and a woman's turning—her languid flight of hair
traveling through frame after frame of memory
where the past turns, its face sparkling like emery,
to open its grace and incredible harm
over my life, and I will never die.

SHEROD SANTOS

Married Love

As they sat and talked beneath the boundary trees
In the abandoned park, neither one mentioning
Her husband, or his wife, it seemed as though
Their summer shadows had detached themselves
In the confusion of those thousand leaves: but no more
Than they could call those shadows back from the air,
Could they ignore the lives they had undone,
And would undo once more, that afternoon,
Before giving in to what they knew, had always known.
And yet, in turning away, what they would say was not
That thing, but something else, that mild excuse
That lovers use of how things might have been
Had they met somewhere else, or in some better time,
Were they less like themselves than what they are.

JULIA ALVAREZ

from 33

"Where are the girls who were so beautiful?"

Where are the girls who were so beautiful?
I don't mean back in the olden days either,
I mean yesterday and the day before
yesterday? Tell me, if you can, where will
I find breathless Vivien or Marilyn,
her skirt blown up? Certainly Natalie,
struggling in the cold waves, deserved to be
fished out when the crew finished and given
her monogrammed beach towel and a hot drink.
How many times didn't we pay good money
to see them saved from worse catastrophes
as they trembled in swimsuits on the brink
of death, Rita and Jean, Lana and Joan,
Frances, Marlene—their names sound like our own.

"Let's make a modern primer for our kids"

Let's make a modern primer for our kids:
A is for Auschwitz; B for Biafra;
Chile; Dachau; El Salvador; F is
the Falklands; Grenada; Hiroshima
stands for H; Northern Ireland for I;
J is for Jonestown; K for Korea;
L for massacres in Lidice; My Lai;
N, Nicaragua; O, Okinawa;
P is the Persian Gulf and Qatar, Q;
Rwanda; Sarajevo—this year's hell;
T is Treblinka and Uganda U;
Vietnam and Wounded Knee. What's left to spell?
An X to name the countless disappeared
when they are dust in Yemen or Zaire.

DANA GIOIA

Sunday Night in Santa Rosa

The carnival is over. The high tents,
the palaces of light, are folded flat
and trucked away. A three-time loser yanks
the Wheel of Fortune off the wall. Mice
pick through the garbage by the popcorn stand.
A drunken giant falls asleep beside
the juggler, and the Dog-Faced Boy sneaks off
to join the Serpent Lady for the night.
Wind sweeps ticket stubs along the walk.
The Dead Man loads his coffin on a truck.
Off in a trailer by the parking lot
the radio predicts tomorrow's weather
while a clown stares in a dressing mirror,
takes out a box, and peels away his face.

MEDBH McGUCKIAN

Still Life of Eggs

for Sylvia Kelly

You are almost kneeling, a diagonal shoreline
between two harbours, in the house-fostered darkness.
The tilt of your head reflects the arc
of the tablecloth, the curve of the sea.
And if the weather could fling its reds,
greens, blues, and purples across table-tops
(thought upon the unthinking) the blue might stay
a river or a lake, the fraying edges fog.
Like the beginning of a painting you have been
so watched: like an additional storey squeezed
into a steep roof, you freeze
the forever ripening shadows under
your eyebrows and neck into younger stone.
Contained, containing—perfectly alone.

PAUL MULDOON

Why Brownlee Left

Why Brownlee left, and where he went,
Is a mystery even now.
For if a man should have been content
It was him; two acres of barley,
One of potatoes, four bullocks,
A milker, a slated farmhouse.
He was last seen going out to plough
On a March morning, bright and early.

By noon Brownlee was famous;
They had found all abandoned, with
The last rig unbroken, his pair of black
Horses, like man and wife,
Shifting their weight from foot to
Foot, and gazing into the future.

Holy Thursday

They're kindly here, to let us linger so late,
Long after the shutters are up.
A waiter glides from the kitchen with a plate
Of stew, or some thick soup,

And settles himself at the next table but one.
We know, you and I, that it's over,
That something or other has come between
Us, whatever we are, or were.

The waiter swabs his plate with bread
And drains what's left of his wine,
Then rearranges, one by one,
The knife, the fork, the spoon, the napkin,
The table itself, the chair he's simply borrowed,
And smiles, and bows to his own absence.

October 1950

Whatever it is, it all comes down to this;
My father's cock
Between my mother's thighs.
Might he have forgotten to wind the clock?

Cookers and eaters, Fuck the Pope,
Wow and flutter, a one-legged howl,
My sly quadroon, the way home from the pub—
Anything wild or wonderful—

Whatever it is, it goes back to this night,
To a chance remark
In a room at the top of the stairs;
To an open field, as like as not,
Under the little stars.
Whatever it is, it leaves me in the dark.

RITA DOVE

Hades' Pitch

If I could just touch your ankle, he whispers, *there
on the inside, above the bone*—leans closer,
breath of lime and peppers—*I know I could
make love to you.* She considers
this, secretly thrilled, though she wasn't quite
sure what he meant. He was good
with words, words that went straight to the liver.
Was she falling for him out of sheer boredom—
cooped up in this anything-but-humble dive, stone
gargoyles leering and brocade drapes licked with fire?
Her ankle burns where he described it. She sighs
just as her mother aboveground stumbles, is caught
by the fetlock—bereft in an instant—
while the Great Man drives home his desire.

Sonnet in Primary Colors

This is for the woman with one black wing
perched over her eyes: lovely Frida, erect
among parrots, in the stern petticoats of the peasant,
who painted herself a present—
wildflowers entwining the plaster corset
her spine resides in, that flaming pillar—
this priestess in the romance of mirrors.

Each night she lay down in pain and rose
to the celluloid butterflies of her Beloved Dead,
Lenin and Marx and Stalin arrayed at the footstead.
And rose to her easel, the hundred dogs panting
like children along the graveled walks of the garden, Diego's
love a skull in the circular window
of the thumbprint searing her immutable brow.

MARK JARMAN

from *Unholy Sonnets*

9

Someone is always praying as the plane
Breaks up, and smoke and cold and darkness blow
Into the cabin. Praying as it happens,
Praying before it happens that it won't.
Someone was praying that it never happen
Before the first window on Kristallnacht
Broke like a wine glass wrapped in bridal linen.
Before it was imagined, someone was praying
That it be unimaginable. And then,
The bolts blew off and people fell like bombs
Out of their names, out of the living sky.
Surely, someone was praying. And the prayer
Struck the blank face of earth, the ocean's face,
The rockhard, rippled face of facelessness.

14 *In via est cisterna*

All she remembers from her Latin class
Is a phrase she echoes for her granddaughter.
Lately I hear in everything she says
A depth that she covers up with laughter.
In the road is a well. But in her mind
It fills with blanks, like a shaft of sand and pebbles.
A well is in the road. It is profound,
I'm sure, it is a phrase with many levels.
And then, I see one: the woman with five husbands
Met Jesus there. But my mother had only one—
Unless now having lost him she understands
That he was never who she thought, but someone
Who was different men with different women through the years.
In the road is a well. It fills with tears.

ELIZABETH MACKLIN

I Fail to Speak to My Earth, My Desire

Having set my heart on you, I remove it
and set it aside. You my desire,
my table, my solid ground, my own true
surface. A mouse in any corner may try
to come out. A wind may cool and blow
us askew. You my desire are not my
property. You may not ever be so.

You my love, my world. Now, have I set my heart on
you? A trace, a kiss, a print, a small brown
scratch: Do you have a clue? Kind as you are,
I am proud or— Nothing in the whole great house
will show where the heart is now. Nor
will the mouse find comforting crumbs. As if, my ground,
I were still waiting to be shown what it is I am for.

TOM SLEIGH

The Very End

for my Grandmother

My eyes are strange to the print tonight;
Nero, Caligula, their crimes disappear.
Instead, a pair of button-shoes you wore,
False teeth, a veil, a monogrammed bracelet,
Blot the Roman sun with their antiquity;
And risen in its place, you dust or cook,
Read the latest in child psychology,
Your gloved voice threatening, "Wouldn't you like . . ."
Yes, it is miraculous to think of you
At all, what with history droning names
Pricked by the triumvirate, Oblivion,
Epitaph, Farewell. Even to see you
Surface above your facts, the dates marked for birth,
Marriage, death, asks that I float you on my breath.

ROSANNA WARREN

Necrophiliac

More marrow to suck, more elegies
to whistle through the digestive track. So help
me God to another dollop of death,
come on strong with the gravy and black-eyed peas,
slop it all in the transcendental stew
whose vapors rise and shine in the nostrils of heaven.
Distill the belches, preserve the drool as ink:
Death, since you nourish me, I'll flatter you
inordinately. Consumers both, with claws
cocked and molars prompt at the fresh-dug grave,
reaper and elegist, we collaborate
and batten in this strictest of intimacies,
my throat an open sepulchre, my tongue
forever groping grief forever young.

DAVID BAKER

Top of the Stove

And then she would lift her griddle
tool from the kindling bin, hooking one
end through a hole in the cast-iron disk
to pry it up with a turn of her wrist.

Our faces pinked over to watch coal
chunks churn and fizz. This was before
I had language to say so, the flatiron
hot all day by the kettle, fragrance

of coffee and coal smoke over
the kitchen in a mist. What did I know?
Now they've gone. Language remains.
I hear her voice like a lick of flame

to a bone-cold day. Careful, she says.
I hold my head close to see what she means.

PHILLIS LEVIN

Final Request

If I die I will need a cross
To carry me to the next world,
The one I do not believe in.
But a cross will carry me
Anyway. When I meet the dory
That overturns despair—
When he who could not
Let love carry him over

Weeps, finally weeps there,
Where he does not believe
He will go—my arms will be
So cruel. Whether or not
They hold him, whether or not
I want to they will want to.

JOHN BURNSIDE

The Myth of the Twin

Say it moved when you moved:
a softness that rose in the ground
when you walked, or a give in your step,
the substance that Virgil saw
in the shadows under our feet;

and say it was out there, out in the snow,
meshed with the birdsong and light
the way things are real: a blackbird, a scribble of thorns,
a quickening into the moment, the present tense,

and the way that a stumbling or sudden
rooting in authenticity is not
the revelation of a foreign place,
but emptiness, a stillness in the frost,
the silence that stands in the birchwoods, the common soul.

CAROL ANN DUFFY

Prayer

Some days, although we cannot pray, a prayer
utters itself. So, a woman will lift
her head from the sieve of her hands and stare
at the minims sung by a tree, a sudden gift.

Some nights, although we are faithless, the truth
enters our hearts, that small familiar pain;
then a man will stand stock-still, hearing his youth
in the distant Latin chanting of a train.

Pray for us now. Grade I piano scales
console the lodger looking out across
a Midlands town. Then dusk, and someone calls
a child's name as though they named their loss.

Darkness outside. Inside, the radio's prayer—
Rockall. Malin. Dogger. Finisterre.

ROBIN ROBERTSON

Wedding the Locksmith's Daughter

The slow-grained slide to embed the blade
of the key is a sheathing,
a gliding on graphite, pushing inside
to find the ribs of the lock.

Sunk home, the true key slots to its matrix;
geared, tight-fitting, they turn
together, shooting the spring-lock,
throwing the bolt. Dactyls, iambics—

the clinch of words—the hidden couplings
in the cased machine. A chime of sound
on sound: the way the sung note snibs on meaning

and holds. The lines engage and marry now,
their bells are keeping time;
the church doors close and open underground.

KARL KIRCHWEY

Zoo Story

It *could* have been the soul of my dead mother
I recognized quite accidentally
in the eyes of an Asian elephant cow.
That body shrugged toward me like a boulder
set to run downhill. The trunk idled with a listless
delicacy over dirty straw,
pinkly inquisitive. I heard a sigh.
I do not believe in metempsychosis;
yet, in a temple lobed and domed most strangely,
I mourned again, and worshiped after her,
buried in this landslide of a creature,
its crushing, dreamlike step, its slack repose,
its gaze, deep as the past or the hereafter,
swaying through counts of years, steady on me.

DEBORAH LASER

from *Between Two Gardens*

Night shares this day with me, is the rumpled
air about me. All day I go about dressed
in a stubborn dress, pink broadcloth
creased and starched and scented by night.

When I feel its scratch I think of night.
When I smell its slow drying I remember
the distant moon, cat across the yard,
my arms suspended, towels, and it

underneath the maple's stars. On days I want
to hold the dark. I dig in the garden,
tear up dandelions, long to enter the earth.

This is no death wish: I want to blossom
into a maple or an oak. Come, sit between
my shallow roots, lean; but do not pull me up.

JACQUELINE OSHEROW

Yom Kippur Sonnet, with a Line from Lamentations

Can a person atone for pure bewilderment?
For hyperbole? for being wrong
In a thousand categorical opinions?
For never opening her mouth, except too soon?
For ignoring, all week long, the waning moon
Retreating from its haunt above the local canyons,
Signaling her season to repent,
Then deflecting her repentance with a song?
Because the rest is just too difficult to face—
What we are—I mean—in all its meagerness—
The way we stint on any modicum of kindness—
What we allow ourselves—what we don't learn—
How each lapsed, unchanging year resigns us—
Return us, Lord, to you, and we'll return.

JAMES LASDUN

Powder Compact

Twenties, machine-age cloisonné, steel lines
Shimmying through the enamel plaque,
Priced voluptuously—as I wrote the check
My new love surged on its own extravagance—
Nocturnal, businesslike, here was your brisk
Sinuous walk, your pagan/Puritan air—
It was like buying you in miniature . . .
I didn't look inside. A stifling musk
Burst on us as you opened it: the past;
The original owner's scented powder puff—
That's all. I didn't catch *memento mori*
Whispered in her spilt, too intimate dust
Till now, or read in hers, love's epitaph
Still pink and scut-soft in its reliquary.

Plague Years

*There is, it would seem, in the dimensional scale of the world, a kind
of delicate meeting place between imagination and knowledge, a point,
arrived at by diminishing large things and enlarging small ones, that is
intrinsically artistic.*   —VLADIMIR NABOKOV, *SPEAK MEMORY*

Sore throat, persistent cough . . . The campus doctor
Tells me "just to be safe" to take the test.
The clinic protocol seems to insist
On an ironic calm. I hold my fear.
He draws a vial of blood for the City Lab,
I have to take it there, but first I teach
A class on Nabokov. Midway I reach
Into my bag for *Speak Memory*, and grab
The hot bright vial instead. I seem at once
Wrenched from the quizzical faces of my class
Into some silent anteroom of hell:
The "delicate meeting place"; I feel it pounce;
Terror—my life impacted in the glass
My death enormous in its scarlet grail.

KATE LIGHT

Reading Someone Else's Love Poems

is, after all, all we've ever done
for centuries—except write them—but what
a strange thing it is, after all, rose-cheeks and sun-
hair and lips, and underarms, and that little gut
I love to nuzzle on, soft underbelly—oops—
that wasn't what I meant to talk about;
ever since handkerchiefs fell, and hoop-
skirts around ankles swirled
and smiled, lovers have dreamed their loves upon
the pages, courted and schemed and twirled
and styled, hoping that once they'd unfurled their down-
deep longing, they would have their prize—
not the songs of love, but love beneath disguise.

JOE BOLTON

from *Style*

11

I was surprised to find how light I felt
With most of the back of my head missing.
I recall, when I was twelve, French kissing
A girl named Star in the dark of a half-built
Duplex at the edge of our subdivision.
It was twilight. I hear my mother's voice,
My name. Women loved me like licorice.
It took me years to find a decision
I could make; now I want to change my mind.
I want to stand up and say "It's all right"
To the mirror. I want to fall crying
Into my father's arms, ask what happened.
At least I looked good, walking down the street
With all the well-dressed dead, the chic dying.

RAFAEL CAMPO

The Mental Status Exam

What is the color of the mind? Beneath
The cranium it's pinkish grey, with flecks
Of white mixed in. What is the mind's motif?
Depends on what you mean: it's either sex
Or it's a box, release or pessimism.
Remember these three things: ball, sorrow, red.
Count backwards, from one-hundred down by sevens.
What is the color of the mind? It's said
That love can conquer all—interpret, please.
And who's the President? What year is it?
The mind is timeless, dizzy, unscrupulous;
The mind is sometimes only dimly lit.
Just two more silly questions: Can you sing
For us? Do you remember those three things?

MIKE NELSON

Light Sonnet for the Lover of a Dark

I was not much more than a boy in those
days, and of all the half-witted ideas
I had, the one that a woman could mean
everything has come back to haunt me.

She and I went walking and arguing
about her face. Though it was night, the dark
brushed its hair aside, as she brushed her hair
aside, and I clearly saw. It was

what happened in a planetarium
when the lights faded out and the stars came on
and were set turning. Way back. Way back. Fooled
by the illusion so the mystery

could take place. Squinting to make the ceiling
vault again. Just try and forget it.

DANIEL GUTSTEIN

What Can Disappear

"The very structure of it," said Warren, "the very idea. Now,
    think.
Rhyme—yes. Meter—yes. The number of lines—yes, yes, yes,—"
he said, as I got it, it seemed, an eight and a six, an eight and two
    less,
the sestet as an octave minus two. We smiled a moment, then
    drank
down our drafts, and more, and more after those. The dull clinks
our glasses left on the table, in toast, until we slurred—"less and
    loss,
lessen lost." We gave up laughing. Warren went to pay, then to
    piss.
Then I thought: two lines gone—the genius of the sonnet—in a
    blink.

We would never meet again. I would sit at our table and conjure
the very structure of it, the very idea. Meter—yes, yes, and rhyme.
The sestet as an octave minus two—or, *what can disappear*. I mull
the table's quiet grain, my draft (a couple sips short), and I figure
how the loss of a person grows beyond form, magnitude, and time.
How there used to be two glasses rising and falling. Now, the
    lull—

BETH ANN FENNELLY

Poem Not to Be Read at Your Wedding

You ask me for a poem about love
in place of a wedding present, trying to save me
money. For three nights I've laid under
glow-in-the-dark stars I've stuck to the ceiling
over my bed. I've listened to the songs
of the galaxy. Well, Carmen, I would rather
give you your third set of steak knives
than tell you what I know. Let me find you
some other store-bought present. Don't
make me warn you of stars, how they see us
from that distance as miniature and breakable,
from the bride who tops the wedding cake
to the Mary on Pinto dashboards
holding her ripe, red heart in her hands.

JASON SCHNEIDERMAN

The Disease Collector

Odd word: culture, as though this swab cared
About art and music, loved the opera,
Saw the Ballet Russe when Nijinsky still bared
His chest, could quote the illuminata
In the original Italian. As though this petri dish
Were a center of learning, and parents wished
For their children to go there, like Harvard or Yale,
As though a positive answer would not pale
My cheeks, or force me to wholly rearrange
My life around pills and doctor's visits;
Force me to find old lovers and tricks,
Warn that their bodies may too grow strange;
To play the old game of who gave it to whom,
Gently lowering voices, alone in one's room.

ACKNOWLEDGEMENTS

"Night shares this day with me, is the rumpled" from *Between Two Gardens* by Debra Laser. Copyright © Debra Laser, 2001.

"Light Sonnet for the Lover of a Dark" by Mike Nelson. Copyright © Mike Nelson, 2001.

"The Disease Collector" by Jason Alexander Schneiderman. Copyright © Jason Alexander Schneiderman, 2001.

All rights reserved.

Grateful acknowledgement is made for permission to reprint the following copyrighted works:

Julia Alvarez, "Where are the girls who were so beautiful" and "Let's make a modern primer for our kids" from 33 from *Homecoming, Revised Edition* (New York: Plume, 1996). Copyright © 1984, 1996 by Julia Alvarez. Reprinted with permission of Susan Bergholz Literary Services, New York. All rights reserved.

John Ashbery, "Rain Moving In" from *A Wave* (New York: Viking, 1984). Copyright © 1984 by John Ashbery. Reprinted with permission of Georges Borchardt, Inc. for the author.

W. H. Auden, "Who's Who", "Our Bias" and "Brussels in Winter"; "The Door" from *The Quest: A Sonnet Sequence*; XII ("And the age ended, and the last deliverer died"); and XXVII ("Wandering lost upon the mountain of our choice") from *In Time of War*; from *The Collected Poetry of W. H. Auden*. Copyright 1934, 1941, 1945, renewed © 1961 by W. H. Auden. Reprinted with permission of Random House, Inc. and Faber & Faber Ltd.

David Baker, "Top of the Stove" from *The Truth About Small Towns*. Copyright © 1998 by David Baker. Reprinted with permission of the University of Arkansas Press.

George Barker, "To My Mother" from *Selected Poems*. Copyright © 1995 by George Barker. Reprinted with permission of Faber & Ltd.

James K. Baxter, 1 ("The small gray cloudy louse that nests in my beard") from *Jerusalem Sonnets* from *Collected Poems of James K. Baxter*, edited by J. E. Weir. Copyright © 1996 by James K. Baxter. Reprinted with permission of Oxford University press.

John Berryman, 7 ("I've found out why, that day, that suicide"), 15 ("What was Ashore, then? ... Cargoed with Forget") and 36 ("Keep your eyes open when you kiss: do: when") from *Berryman's Sonnets*. Copyright © 1967 by